What people are sa
Celtic Fairies in No

T0284381

Fairy lore of North America, overlooked by scholars for a while, is re-capturing the public's interest. In this book Morgan Daimler lifts the curtain and brings into the spotlight the Celtic fairies – their lore, traditions, and their very presence – on the North American continent. The story material gathered here, many of it coming from primary sources, reveals a rich landscape where old and new, native and imported beliefs interact to create the contemporary body of North American fairy lore. Throughout *Celtic Fairies in North America*, scholarship, personal gnosis, pertinent information and practical suggestions are in perfect balance making this a most valuable asset to scholars and spiritual seekers alike. Morgan argues poignantly about the validity of personal gnosis even when it does not align precisely to the older lore. Throughout the book Morgan makes the case for people trusting themselves in accepting their own fairy experiences as genuine because personal gnosis further shapes fairy lore. *Celtic Fairies in North America* stands out as bold, thorough, both instructive and encouraging for those who for one reason or another cross paths with the Celtic fairies on this continent.

Daniela Simina, author of *Where Fairies Meet: Parallels between Irish and Romanian Fairy Traditions* and *A Fairy Path: The Memoir of a Young Fairy Seer in Training*

Author Morgan Daimler turns an analytical eye to the question of Celtic fae, or Celtic-influenced fairies, in North America. This delightful book examines the fairies and fae spirits – and common superstitions about them – from Newfoundland and Nova Scotia to the Appalachians; and takes a peek at similar spirits in Mexico. Using historical references and contemporary anecdotes, Daimler

paints a picture of a diaspora of the fae folk, who traveled with immigrants from Ireland, England or Breton, to become settled and recognized in America. Daimler's book, written in an analytical but comfortable style, brings the story of the Celtic fairies who came to the New World to life. Highly recommended.
Miles Batty, author of *Teaching Witchcraft*

I love Morgan Daimler's books, with their thorough and reliable research, clearly delivered, which has a habit of challenging cherished but mistaken perceptions. *Celtic Fairies in North America* is a book I craved without knowing it. Living in Canada but immersed in Irish lore and legend, I sometimes feel bereft of a mythology I can claim as deeply my own: I'm not Irish; I'm not indigenous Canadian. But here I learn about the continuation and evolution in my own land (and the US and Mexico) of the folklore of my ancestors, and about the influences that came to bear on them. Daimler delivers this in a non-judgmental way, just as they let reports of modern experiences of fairies stand on their own merits. I wholeheartedly recommend this short and pithy text.
Mael Brigde author of *A Brigit of Ireland Devotional*

If you want to get your bearings in the wild flurry of information and opinions about Themselves in North America, this book is the resource you're looking for. Through meticulous research, Daimler organizes and clarifies a huge mass of information, distilling it down for ease of understanding – at least, as much as we're ever likely to understand the Good People. Daimler offers plenty of historical background as well as present-day anecdotes about fairy encounters that anchor the narrative in the now. The research is thorough, the evidence compelling: Themselves are here!
Laura Perry, author of *Labrys and Horns: An Introduction to Modern Minoan Paganism*

Morgan Daimler's *Celtic Fairies of North America* offers an insightful journey into the transatlantic migration of fairy lore, skillfully challenging the notion that European fairy beliefs had minimal influence in North America. Through meticulous research and engaging narrative, Daimler highlights the die-hard impact of these beliefs, especially within Irish and Scottish diasporas in Canada and the United States. The book maps the journey of these fairy beliefs and their remarkable adaptability, showcasing how they have been integral to North American folklore. While exploring the intersection of folklore, migration, and cultural identity, Daimler presents a mosaic of stories and historical contexts as well as experiences from people today, making it an enlightening read for enthusiasts of folklore and cultural studies. *Celtic Fairies of North America* is not just a study of mythological beings; it's a testament to the enduring nature of cultural beliefs of fairies and their ability to cross oceans and transform within new landscapes. This work is as much about the resilience and evolution of cultural identity as it is about the enchanting world of fairies.

Mat Auryn, author of *Psychic Witch* and *Mastering Magick*

Pagan Portals

Celtic Fairies in North America

Pagan Portals

Celtic Fairies in North America

Morgan Daimler

MOON
BOOKS

London, UK
Washington, DC, USA

CollectiveInk

First published by Moon Books, 2024
Moon Books is an imprint of Collective Ink Ltd.,
Unit 11, Shepperton House, 89 Shepperton Road, London, N1 3DF
office@collectiveinkbooks.com
www.collectiveinkbooks.com
www.moon-books.net

For distributor details and how to order please visit the 'Ordering' section on our website.

Text copyright: Morgan Daimler 2023

ISBN: 978 1 80341 434 8
978 1 80341 435 5 (ebook)
Library of Congress Control Number: 2023949962

A CIP catalogue record for this book is available from the British Library.

Design: Lapiz Digital Services

UK: Printed and bound by CPI Group (UK) Ltd, Croydon, CR0 4YY
Printed in North America by CPI GPS partners

We operate a distinctive and ethical publishing philosophy in all areas of our business, from our global network of authors to production and worldwide distribution.

Contents

Dedicated to everyone who has ever asked me
if Celtic fairies can be found across the Atlantic

With thanks to Robert Schreiwer for suggesting sources in an online discussion, and pointing me towards some of the Pennsylvania Deutsch thoughts on the subject; to Daniel Harms for assistance in some of the academic research around indigenous spirits; and to Sabina Magliocco for suggesting some research leads as well. Thanks as well to Brandon Weston for assistance with the Appalachian material.

Huge appreciation to the people who kindly responded to my request for modern fairy encounters.

I'd also like to extend my deep gratitude to Chris Woodyard and Simon Young for their previous and ongoing work in researching both modern fairy encounters as well as documenting historic accounts in the United States. This book wouldn't have been written nearly as quickly or concisely without that existing material to work from and build off of.

Author's Note

This book is the result of many years of people asking me whether or not we could find Celtic fairies in North America. I finally decided the best option would be to write a book on the subject and address everything all in one place. Hopefully this helps give people the answers they are looking for and offers a better understanding of the way that beliefs move and change, and the way that belief in spirits travel with communities.

Every book ultimately reflects the biases of the author and for me these are not only folkloric beliefs found across the last several hundred years but also represent a reality for people who believe in them. I don't attempt to offer rational explanations for belief in fairies because I think that the beliefs reflect a perceptual reality. This view undoubtedly colours my opinions here but I have done my best to be objective in what is shared and I want everyone, no matter what your viewpoints are, to find some value here.

I believe that America is full of beliefs in a wide variety of spirits from many cultures. I know that my grandfather, when he came over from Cork, never gave up the practice of pouring out a bit of his beer for the Good Neighbours whenever he drank, and even on American soil never doubted that the Good People would cause trouble if not given their due. This is a belief that has been firmly ingrained in me as well. My own experiences since childhood involved both spirits undoubtedly native to this continent as well as those that seem to have immigrated or otherwise been shaped by the beliefs of the Irish who came to this place, as well as a wide array of other cultures. America is more than just a melting pot of human cultures but in my experience is also a melting pot of spirits, containing a wide diversity, and this diversity seems to go back hundreds of years, since colonization first began making permanent settlements on this continent.

I personally favour using APA citation in my writing and so throughout this book when a source is being cited you will see the name of the author and date of the book in parenthesis after that. I have also included end notes expanding on points that don't fit neatly into the larger text but are important to touch on, and which I hope will help clarify certain points for readers.

I hope that this book can serve as a good introduction to the idea of fairies as both stationary and travelling beings, and to the concepts around community belief and diasporic folklore.

Foreword

In writing *Celtic Fairies in North America*, Morgan Daimler brings to the table a weighty argument in the debate about whether fairies from Celtic language-speaking cultures migrated to North America.

For some, fairies are connected to geographical areas almost in the same way as boulders and ancient trees are fixtures in a landscape. Others argue in defence of fairies having agency, agendas, and capability to relocate just as humans do. Theosophy and the Victorian era popularized fairies as nature spirits bound to natural settings. However, traditional lore from Western Europe talks about fairies changing houses at specific times throughout the year and traveling on fairy roads known only to themselves. Furthermore, there are tales of humans accompanying fairies on escapades to foreign lands, whether by force or consent. But why would fairies travel from Europe all the way to the Americas? And would they relocate to the New World alongside migrating humans?

To argue in favour of Celtic fairies' presence in North America, Morgan Daimler adopts primarily an ethnographic approach, including anecdotal material, and also making reference to entire collections of such material. Further, Morgan analyses how the intertwining of contemporary fairy-related experiences and old traditions paints the picture of Celtic fairies in North America today. The book provides plenty of examples that illustrate the idea that not just beliefs, but fairies themselves accompanied the European immigrants to North America. The material cited throughout is rich and includes numerous primary sources. With flawless logic and solid argumentation, Morgan Daimler demonstrates that the picture of Celtic fairies in North America, as scarce or non-existing, is inaccurate. The stories collected in this volume substantiate the beliefs in fairies and in a sense document their permanence in the North American cultural landscape.

Morgan Daimler delves into explaining how native and imported beliefs interacted with one another leading to the emergence of new nuances and even entirely new beliefs. We see that older stories of fairy encounters are more in line with the lore native to areas where the settlers came from. And we can't help but notice that recent encounters diverge from older lore to a smaller or larger extent. Morgan points out that sometimes, in contemporary fairy encounters, personal gnosis is different from the old and familiar perspectives. This change in the frame of reference, leaves humans disoriented in the aftermath of such encounters. For all those in need to process or somehow make sense of fairy-related experiences, the book offers an entire section with pertinent information and practical recommendations.

A treasure-trove of stories of real experiences that people had with fairies in recent years paint the picture of ongoing and vibrant fairy activity in North America today. Morgan Daimler speaks of the interaction between indigenous and imported fairy beliefs with respect and sensitivity in regard to cultural appropriation. North American culture is a colourful tapestry where local and imported traditions weave harmoniously to create a homogenous design, yet individual threads remain clearly discernible through their texture and colour. People indigenous to North America have their own distinct lore about beings who are not entirely dissimilar to the Celtic fairies. Morgan points out the distinction between Celtic fairies and indigenous fairy-beings, and discusses the permanence of Celtic fairy lore and the influences it may have absorbed from interacting with the native folklore. This is important information for anyone searching for answers in folklore and cultural anthropology. Not only are the North American fairies different from their European counterparts, but they also differ across the various geographical regions on the American continent. There is beauty in diversity: this holds true for American culture as a whole and for the Celtic fairies themselves who are part and parcel of it.

Old and newly emerged cultural trends defined fairies, and such defining affects people's personal experience of fairies. By engaging with fairy lore, we actively participate in the making of what future generations will appreciate as the fairy folklore of their time. This is a huge responsibility for us to shoulder. Thankfully, Morgan Daimler's book offers invaluable information to assist us through this process, in our role of co-creators of lore and traditions side by side with the Celtic fairies from North America.

Daniela Simina, author of *Where Fairies Meet Parallels between Irish and Romanian Fairy Traditions*, and *A Fairy Path: The Memoir of a Young Fairy Seer in Training*

Introduction

If you had asked someone who believed in fairies a hundred years ago if there were any of these beings outside the traditional Celtic language speaking cultures the answer would likely have been a definitive yes. But today the subject has become controversial, with much debate about where, exactly, one might find these beings. This book is going to look at all the evidence, historic and modern, for the presence of belief in European fairies across North America. Whether or not the reader chooses to believe that these beings can or do exist outside Ireland and the UK is up to each individual, however, I think there is value in sharing the heritage of folklore that can be found with that opinion. These are beliefs that were carried from their places of origin to new territory and were passed on through diasporic[1] communities, although often with changes from the originals becoming evident over time.

I do want to state at the outset that while I will be discussing various beliefs about fairies across the last few centuries, I'm not going to be getting into a discussion of whether fairies are culturally specific or general – in other words I'm not going to argue for or against the ideas that fairies manifest uniquely to different cultures versus the idea that fairies are a universal concept that every culture applies different names to. To dig into that conversation would require an entirely separate book and a much wider scope of discussion. For our purposes here we'll be looking at beliefs across North America – including Canada, the United States, and Mexico – that can be traced back to Europe or which overlap significantly or seem to be a blend of beliefs influenced by European idea around fairies, particularly from the Celtic language speaking cultures of Ireland, Scotland, Wales, Cornwall, the Isle of Man, and Brittany, and to a lesser degree Iberia. Perforce there will also be some crossover with related continental and English beliefs as at points it becomes difficult to entirely separate out each influence on a belief.[2] These beliefs should also be understood as attached to specific communities and not as ubiquitous across North America, and while we can, as I will show, find belief in European fairies in America these beliefs are usually localized rather than general.

I will also not offer any judgement on the veracity of anecdotal accounts. If a person relates a story in which they feel that what they were experiencing was a fairy, then it will be taken as such. In later chapters I will be offering examples of such anecdotes and folk lore across the last 400 or so years, up to today, and these will be offered as they are without any interpretation or analysis. These accounts do all represent genuine experiences by the people relating them and as such the reader should at least put them in the context of that belief, whether or not you share it. In other words, these are experiences that these people truly believe occurred, not stories made up to entertain an audience.

Before we dive into various areas of North America and their fairy beliefs, we must start by clearly defining what we are and aren't discussing here. European fairies are the focus of this work but they are not the totality of the subject, nor the only spirits found in belief across North America. Our focus here, however, will be exclusively – as much as that is possible – on imported beliefs of what we will be calling fairies. The term fairy itself has been used in English for around 600 years and was originally a more general term for certain types of spirits; it was used synonymously with elf, goblin, incubus, and imp. In the last century, and more so the last several decades, the word fairy has been narrowed down to mean something far more specific and particular but in this book, it will be used in the older more general sense, as defined in 1976 by folklorist Katherine Briggs, of fairies as anything supernatural that isn't a ghost, angel, or demon. This more general view has become somewhat controversial now and is often debated for various reasons, particularly in academic usage, but nonetheless it is the most accurate term for use in this book. This is in part because any alternative general term will present its own issues[3] and in part because most people recognize the word fairy and have some idea of what it implies.

What then is a fairy? It is sometimes easier to say what fairies aren't than to clarify what they are, but what we can say for certain, based on the long-term understandings of what fairies are, is that they are beings of the Otherworld, literally 'of Fairy'. These are beings who may interact with the human world and the people in it but who also exist in and perhaps come from a very different place. That place is understood in many ways, and like the beings themselves can be difficult to define or explain;[4] to some people it's a spiritual world, to others a different plane of existence, to others a connected dimension to our world, to yet others it's a reality that is just one step off from our own perceptions. And that place is the home or origin of the beings who we call fairies. Like any world it encompasses a variety of beings and each one is understood in its own way and has its own possible connection to humanity, mythology, or wider belief. Some of them are what we might now call nature spirits. Some of them are understood to be human dead, taken and transformed into Otherworldly beings. Some, like the Tuatha De Danann turned Aos Sidhe, are pagan Gods. And some are none of these things because no one category or explanation fits all of them. The best way to understand what fairies are is to appreciate the nuances. There is no simple answer. Rather, what we see is a diverse grouping that encompasses an array of Otherworldly spirits which we label fairies for convenience. Hundreds, if not thousands, of different kinds of named and even unnamed types of beings fall into this wide category and it makes sense that there is no easy way to understand them all as a whole beyond the broadest strokes.

When most people hear the word fairy, they immediately associate it with the Celtic language speaking cultures of Ireland, Scotland, Wales, Cornwall, the Isle of Man, and Brittany, although England also has a rich history of fairy belief and, of course, originated the term fairy (from the French). Each of those named countries or places has its own terms for these beings in their own languages but for the sake of simplicity here we will be using the term fairy except in situations where the folklore itself is more specific; this reflects the long and muddy use of the word throughout history and within diasporic communities. Most of what we will be looking at across this book will be these Celtic fairies, however, on occasion there will be some crossover with closely related beliefs from other parts of Western Europe.

We will not be discussing indigenous spirits under the umbrella term of fairy, as they should be understood as a distinct set of beliefs. There is a rich tradition of spirit belief indigenous to the Americas, which is complex and specific to different cultures, and which may sometimes overlap with the European beliefs that arrived later or more often stand apart from them. Indigenous spirits may sometimes be called fairies in English but it is best to avoid that direct association as it causes confusion and creates inaccurate assumptions. I prefer to either use the term that the culture in question calls them, for example, the Makiawisug among the Mohegans and Pequots, or to say 'fairy-like' as a general comparative term. While there may be and often are many similarities between these beliefs and European ones using the English language term perpetuates colonization of these beliefs and layers on meanings from English fairy beliefs that do not apply. For those interested in indigenous beliefs I encourage people to learn about the place they live and what culture preceded colonization there, and then find respectful ways to learn more about the beliefs of those peoples regarding spirit beings. I will note though that over the last 400 years there has been both an exchange of beliefs across cultures in contact with each other and in some situations perhaps a blurring of dividing lines or confusion of beliefs, where something may be incorrectly attributed to a group only to then be passed on in that form. In some areas, particularly the north east, it can be difficult to separate out the roots of beliefs or decide which culture was influencing the other.

Chapter 1

Fairies outside Europe

It is widely accepted by many folklorists and academics that European fairy beliefs had little impact in North America historically and didn't leave a notable impression on immigrant populations of the diaspora. I believe that this is perpetuating a misunderstanding of the folk beliefs, in which the limited material we can find today is being viewed as too insignificant to be noted and therefore dismissed as non-existent. However, while it is certainly much less than we have for other areas of belief there is evidence of folk belief in fairies across communities in North America, most prominently among the Irish and Scottish populations of Newfoundland Canada, and the Northeastern and Appalachian areas of the United States. Or as Woodyard and Young put it in the introduction of their article *Three Notes and a Handlist of North American Fairies*:

> "...in the last generation, some local studies have shown that there may have been more European fairylore in nineteenth and twentieth century America than has been previously appreciated." (Woodyard & Young, 2019, page 56).

This material forms the basis to understand the history of fairy belief in North America and shows that while examples may be sparse the concepts have deep roots.

In this chapter we are going to explore some of the arguments around the idea of fairies travelling across the ocean and the general evidence to support it. In later chapters we'll look at the folk beliefs around fairies in Canada, the United States, and Mexico, and then we will expand into popculture fairies in North America. All of these are important aspects of exploring this subject and each is essential in a different way. While I am taking a more ethnographic approach to this book than I have in most of my others[5] this book isn't in itself meant to be a study of the beliefs we're discussing; rather the beliefs are going to be used to demonstrate the widespread presence of fairies in the stories and experiences of diasporic groups.

The crux of the wider debate is the question: can fairies move beyond their traditional places? This question results in three main approaches or arguments:

1. Fairies are found globally but known by different names in different places; i.e., there is only one group of Otherworldly beings that exist and manifest around the globe but different groups understand them through specific cultural lenses.
2. Fairies are an extremely specific type of being tied to geographic locations. This idea hinges on fairies as, firstly, unique to Celtic language speaking areas, and secondly as tied intrinsically to physical locations in the human world.
3. Fairies exist as independent spirit beings who can be attached to a place or to a person/community and who, like humans or some other types of spirits, can go where they choose, within certain contexts.

I should probably add to this a fourth option which is that all of our understandings of these beings are limited to and by our own cultural lenses and we can never really know the answer to the above question. However, those three main views are the ones that I have found to dominate in discussions of whether fairies, as such, can be found outside of Europe.

By the first view they can be found anywhere but will be called by different names in different cultures; this view is somewhat less popular today than it may have been previously and does receive some pushback for bordering on cultural appropriation by removing the nuances in belief that exist between each different groups understanding of fairies. It also risks homogenising these globally diverse spirits into one group which, labelled as fairies, can result in inappropriate assumptions being made about them. For our purposes here I am presenting it for the reader's consideration without judgement but with an understanding of the criticisms it faces.

The second view is the one used to argue against Celtic fairies being found or even possibly existing anywhere outside traditionally Celtic language speaking areas. Through this understanding fairies are not a cultural phenomenon or folk belief but are a geographic phenomenon which is bound to and limited to the location of origin.

The third view is the one which we will be exploring in this book, as we look across the last 400 or so years of folk belief in diaspora communities in North America.

As the idea of fairies being limited to specific locations has become quite common, perhaps first we should look at some of the arguments against the Good Folk travelling as well as counterarguments to those points.

Are fairies tied to geography or specific locations? The main argument here is that fairies, of various types, are strongly connected to or tied to specific places in the human world and are unable to travel far from those places.

In Irish folk belief we find fairy roads or paths, which are believed to be the invisible routes that fairies use to travel, often from one fairy hill to another. In Scottish belief there is the idea that fairies move their homes on specific days, aligned with the traditional times to pay rent. There are also a range of stories which mention fairies crossing from one country to another such as we find in Douglas Hyde's *Beside the Fire* in the story

'Guleesh Na Guss Dubh'; while this is a story not an anecdote it is based in the wider idea that fairies can go to different countries if they choose to. We also find stories of fairies leaving a place if they are driven out by church bells, the railroad, or the clear cutting of a forest (Briggs, 1976).

Can fairies cross water/running water? The main argument here is that we have folklore which says that fairies don't or won't cross running water. Crossing water is suggested as a protection against them as well as a way to escape them when necessary. In most of these examples a person crosses a bridge or body of water while being chased by a fairy of some kind and the fairy stops pursuing the person.

While we do find stories of fairies who appear unable to cross streams or bodies of water there are also a multitude of stories about fairies who do cross water. In the story *'Guleesh na Guss Dhu'* in Douglas Hyde's *Beside the Fire* the human main character joins a fairy host and crosses the sea to Europe, for one example, and in Patricia Lysaght's book *The Banshee* she relates a story of a man chased by a banshee who continues following him even after he leaps across a stream. In *Fairy Faith in Celtic Countries* Evans-Wentz relays a story about a man who had a fairy lover who became too draining and so he chose to flee across the ocean, yet later he wrote back to his family that this ploy failed and the fairy was with him still in his new country. There are two examples of Irish stories where fairies carry a person from Ireland to the United States for a short period before returning them back to Ireland, demonstrating that fairies can cross the ocean if they choose to (Woodyard & Young, 2019). We also find a story from Prince Edward Island, Canada, where a man who was kidnapped and then returned by the fairies describes being carried across the ocean to Europe then back; on the return trip he was cajoled to agree to go with the fairies again and every time he refused was dipped into the waves until he finally agreed (Woodyard & Young, 2019). In all of these examples it is clear that the fairies involved were not hindered by bodies of water, including the ocean.

Historically migrant populations have always carried their beliefs with them, rather than seeing their beliefs as immovably anchored to specific places. We can see this if we look back at the original movement of the Celtic culture[6] which brought certain Gods to new lands; these deities are often called "pan-Celtic" because they can be found in some form in most or all Celtic cultures. We can also see this, for example, in the way the Dál Riada Irish brought some of the Tuatha Dé Danann to Scotland where the beliefs took root and blossomed into a different form. A non-Celtic example is the way that the Norse brought their Gods and understanding of spirits with them to Iceland, where there was and is a rich folk belief in beings like the álfar and huldufolk. People's beliefs don't cease to exist when they relocate their communities.[7] When we look at the range of folk beliefs, we might conclude that while some types of spirits are indeed sedentary, others are pulled or drawn to where the people who honour and offer to them are or otherwise choose to follow humans to new locations.

So, there's certainly historical precedent for the idea of Gods and spirits going with a population as it moves, or at least of the people retaining their beliefs which are then usually melded or slowly integrated into existing local beliefs. Although I do believe that it is important to journey to those places and experience the land of those stories, as they are often strongly tied to these specific places, the bulk of evidence across folk belief indicates that a variety of spirits are present anywhere they choose to be and can create connections to any place where they are honoured. One school of thought on this is simply that the Otherworldly folk appear to people in ways that those people can best understand; another view is that the spirits are influenced by the belief of the people. Both of these assume a certain fluidity and malleability to the fairies which has become a popular view due to theosophy's influence but is less clear in folk belief. The main support for the idea that fairies can take on guises to suit what a viewer expects are based in the wider belief in fairies having a type of magic called glamour which can affect a human's perceptions. We see this prominently in the fairy midwife motif, where the human midwife gains the ability to see through fairy illusions and realizes the entire reality she has been perceiving – usually a very luxurious home, is actually false.[8] In the same way the idea that fairies are influenced by human belief is a complex one, which can be both supported and argued against within the range of evidence. In some stories it's clear that people are seeing or perceiving fairies in ways they did not expect or couldn't anticipate, including sceptics having intense fairy experiences, but in other cases we do see a clear evolution of fairies as they are perceived. An example of that which we will discuss in depth in Chapter 5 would be both wings and pointed ears.

When the Norse settled Iceland, they believed that they found álfar and huldufolk there just as there had been in their old home territories. The Wild Hunt is seen in American skies just as in European, although they are more commonly known as "Ghost Riders" here, and the folklore is slightly different. The areas of America heavily settled by the Irish and Scottish, like Appalachia, have local folklore that includes traditionally Irish spirits like the Banshee and Will'o'the'Wisp. In a folklore journal from 1894, we find an article about an area of Massachusetts' local belief in fairies and pixies, the former being lucky and the latter malicious. In all these examples, which we will discuss in depth later, the people clearly felt it perfectly natural and normal to see and experience the types of Otherworldly spirits from their homelands even in these new places.

Dennis Boyer relays the opinion of a professor in Germany in his book *Once Upon a Hex*, who talks of how those who emigrated to the US took some spirits with them, going so far as to say that Germany was the poorer for the loss:

> "'It was that protective capacity the emigrants took with them. They took our best spirits, our ghosts of laughter, and our healing presences. And the last century makes it obvious that we were left more vulnerable when we lost these things.'
>
> 'We had stone quarry spirits and woodsmen spirits, spirits of the rye and barley fields, ghosts of grist mills and blacksmith forges, and even a turnip spirit. They all went to Pennsylvania...'"
> (Boyer, 2004)

Chapter 2

Canada

We will begin by looking at folk beliefs from Canada, specifically eastern Canada where Irish and Scottish influence was strongest. I chose to organize the chapters by geography, north to south, but we could equally argue this structure goes from the strongest folklore to the more obscure because Canada is without question the main repository of fairy folk belief both since colonization and today. As such this chapter will be a general overview of the Candain material, highlighting some of the more interesting stories, but cannot possibly offer a comprehensive look at the subject.

One initial piece of evidence we can look at in Canada is place names based on the word fairy, which can be found in Newfoundland and Nova Scotia (Woodyard & Young, 2019). Place names which incorporate the word fairy or related terms, including hob, are seen as an indication of folk belief in that area and normally have attached stories, anecdotal accounts, or legends to explain the name. The occurrence of fairy-based place names in North America should at the least show a holdover of the concepts from the countries of origin of those who colonized there. Beyond place names Woodyard & Young also documented a variety of fairy accounts from across Canada, including stories of banshees, elves, tommyknockers, gnomes, and fairies;[9] there is at least one changeling adjacent story in Montreal, when a woman who feared being stolen by the fairies eventually committed infanticide (Woodyard & Young, 2019).

The 2018 Fairy Census includes 19 accounts from Canada, from Alberta, British Columbia, Manitoba, Nova Scotia, Ontario, and Quebec. These included both classic examples of fairy beings including gnomes and human-like figures as well as more modern expressions including disembodied lights and small insect-like people. One of the more classic examples occurs on page 152:

"The faeries I experienced were not so much wee folk as in the Victorian illustrations but movement and mist that seemed to form figures. They appeared in two places down by the cedar tree in between its huge roots which grew beside the pond and spring. They stood quietly and gracefully adult sized if not taller." (Young, 2018).

The fairy Census also offers accounts of items being taken and recovered and of lost time during fairy experiences. This account from Ontario is particularly interesting as it involves children dancing in a fairy ring and seeming to disappear for several hours:

"Me and my best friend at age eight were in the countryside for a family barbecue in the fall. Me and her decided to go play in the large woods that evening (just as the sun was starting to set) behind the house because all of the other kids were doing it. We had wandered maybe three minutes into the woods (we could still hear the party faintly) when we came across a ring of mushrooms. I had heard of these being somehow connected to fairies so me and my friend danced around the inside of it for a couple of minutes. When nothing seemed to happen, we left the circle to continue playing. But when we stepped out of the circle, the warm sunset lighting suddenly faded to the point where it was almost pitch black, and we heard our names being called out. We ran towards the voice and found most of the family looking for us. We had apparently been gone for hours. They couldn't see or hear us even though we were a few minutes from the party in a relatively undense part of the forest, and their hunting dog couldn't smell us." (Young, 2018, p 156).

This is largely in line with European fairy lore about fairy rings, particularly French, which allows for the dancer to leave without much difficulty, in contrast to elsewhere where dancing in a fairy ring would require rescue or a person risked being lost forever.

Most Canadian accounts from the Fairy Census are either neutral or benevolent in tone but there is one from Manitoba that is decidedly neither:

> "*I awoke in my bed to find myself surrounded by tiny men dressed in brown holding spears. They did not speak but I was aware that if I moved or cried out that they would stab me. I could not move, and did not cry out. When they finally 'left' I felt that I had passed some test, and that I would not be taken. It is a very strong memory. I believed that my home in the country was surrounded by good fairies, who lived in the trees, but these were malevolent...*" (Young, 2018, p 154).

The person telling the story was a child when it occurred in the 1980s but remembered the event clearly even many years later. The account is clearly more dangerous and echoes older stories of children being stolen by fairies as well as stories of people being elf-shot in order to take them into the fairy world. While that more commonly occurred with cows there are stories of humans experiencing it as well, where the human would be pricked or struck and then pine away or sicken rapidly, with the belief being that they were stolen by the fairies.

These examples represent oral traditions that have been passed down for hundreds of years, sometimes adapted from the European versions sometimes reflecting the European beliefs closely. They also often demonstrate a blending of Irish, Scottish, and French influences as well as indigenous, particularly Mi'kmaq, beliefs. In some areas one source dominates while in others they blend to a greater degree. Below we will look at three particular areas with a higher amount of both historic and modern folklore.

Newfoundland

Newfoundland is an area that has a particularly significant amount of fairy belief that has survived, due to the large diasporic communities settled there. Barbara Rieti has written an entire book about fairy belief in Newfoundland, titled *Strange Terrain*[10] so I will only offer a summary of the material here. This abundance of fairy folklore has made Newfoundland notable to folklorists as it stands in stark contrast to the usual assumption that there are no fairies in North America, an assumption that was long held as true despite available material to the contrary. Newfoundland was considered an anomaly due to its strong Irish diaspora which continued their folk beliefs even in a new country (Narvaez, 1991).

The fairies of Newfoundland are closer to the ones of Ireland and Scotland than perhaps any we find elsewhere, with the beliefs in Newfoundland very close to, if not in some cases identical to, the European ones. The cultures have remained so similar, in fact, the Irish folklorist Michael Fortune, on staying in Newfoundland for a month, remarked that he felt he was still at home due to the similar turns of phrase and use of some Irish language terms (Barrett, 2019; Fortune, 2019). Dr Jenny Butler of University College Cork has studied the connections and similarities between Irish and Newfoundland fairy belief and written two papers on the subject *Fairy legends and landscape: a comparative analysis between Ireland and Newfoundland* and *Ireland and Newfoundland fairy folklore: migratory legends and identity politics* as well as created a short documentary on the topic. There is little doubt that Irish folklore has continued in a particularly strong way in Newfoundland.

One aspect of folk belief which has carried over is 'the blast', which would more usually be called elf-shot or the fairy stroke elsewhere. The blast is a sudden affliction, pain, tumour, or blindness that effects a person who is believed to have offended the fairies. Rieti in her article *The Blast in Newfoundland Fairy Tradition* repeats several second-hand accounts from people who had known the afflicted person and witnessed at least a portion of the events, which happened in the 20th century. The first woman tells a story about a man who was looking for cows in the woods and was struck in the eye by an invisible force which left him blind, another man described someone drinking from a brook and being struck in the face which caused pain and then several items forced their way through his skin, including stones and sticks, leaving him disfigured (Rieti, 1991). The blast having this effect, that is causing foreign items to be found beneath the skin, is a common feature of it in Newfoundland and a less common (but occurring) feature of European elf-shot and fairy stroke stories. Rieti suggests several possible medical explanations for this phenomenon including teratoma and osteomyelitis but our focus here is on the stories themselves and the persistence of belief they demonstrate, not in trying to explain them. The blast sometimes also occurs when a person defies the fairies, as we see in another story that Rieti repeats of a woman to whom the fairies offered a drink; when she refused, they threw the cup at her causing a boil which eventually ruptured and produced a variety of foreign objects. Rieti's article relates more than a dozen of these anecdotal accounts, sometimes having been witnessed by the storyteller sometimes having been passed down over years.

Another aspect of Newfoundland folklore that is similar to that found in Europe is the theme of fairies stealing a person, although in Newfoundland the person is more likely to return within hours or days, whereas the European stories often feature people who are never seen again. In Newfoundland this was most notable among women and children who went to gather berries, despite going out in groups it was not unheard of for a person to disappear only to re-appear later saying they had been with the fairies. The belief was so widespread that it was taken very seriously by parents who would warn children to be especially careful and to turn their clothes if they felt they were being misled or carry silver or some bread which had been marked with the sign of the cross, as the fairies would avoid that[11] (Narvaez, 1991).

> *"By far the [greatest risk] was the "fairies" ... once they had you in their power they could keep you in a trance for days...there were many instances of "fairy-taking" in my town..."* (Narvaez, 1991, p 343).

Narvaez records two dozen accounts of fairy abduction stories in Newfoundland across the 20th century including several first-hand accounts by people who describe either being taken or losing time which their families attributed to fairy abduction.

Not directly connected to the Irish or Scottish diaspora but a portion of fairy belief in Canada, including Newfoundland, was strongly influenced by French folklore and belief has survived there through that lens. Because portions of France, specifically Brittany, are considered Celtic I am including this here. In these areas fairies are referred to by the French term 'Lutin' and are particularly know for creating complex knots and tangles often referred to as elf-knots or fairy-knots; these mats can also appear on humans and are believed to be a sign of fairy presence. In horses it indicates that the animal has been taken out and ridden by the fairies who tangle the mane to create stirrups for themselves (Butler, 1991; McLarty, 2022). It was believed that if a horse had such elf-locks or mats they shouldn't be untangled or cut out of the mane but left as they were to avoid angering the lutins, and a man being interviewed by Gary Butler in his article *The Lutin Tradition in French-Newfoundland Culture* said that when his mare was afflicted with such tangles, he was unable to untangle them even when he tried (Butler, 1991). The concept is directly rooted in French belief from Brittany and Normandy and its occurrence in Eastern Canada is tied to oral tales passed down from older French settlers. Butler interviewed a variety of French speaking people in Newfoundland who discussed the lutins and their penchant for braiding horses' manes, but most disavowed the belief themselves, describing it as something their parents had held true with only one, Emile Benoit, speaking of them as a current reality. Benoit described these beings as small, human-like but with wings like those of a bat, and related a story of his own horse having its mane tangled into three distinct braids which he described as about four inches long, unfinished, and extremely difficult to untangle. Another of Butler's interviewees, John White, told a story about a man who had left a bag of oats out in his stable which the lutin knocked over; the fairy hadn't picked all the oats up before the man returned and saw him although Mr White was unclear on what had happened at that point. It was an old protection against these beings to leave out a container of grain, peas, ashes, or some other small item which the lutin would knock over and then be obligated to pick up one item at a time until it was so frustrated that it left and didn't return (Butler, 1991).

Nova Scotia

The belief in lutins and elf-locks can be found in Nova Scotia just as in Newfoundland. While this belief has faded from its previous prominence it does still exist, as demonstrated in the article *Behind the Fairy Door: A Look at Fairy Lore in Nova Scotia* where someone interviewed in 2022 discussed the idea of lutin tangling horses' manes. Placing a silver coin in water the horse drank from was suggested in folk belief as a cure for these mats (Fraser, 1975). Lutins were said to be mischievous, small people very similar to some understandings of the Irish fairy folk. They were said to appear at dusk with a noise like bird wings and wheels and people singing and talking, in some cases causing so much uproar that people nearby could find no peace except to move their house (Fraser, 1975).

Besides lutin we also find the more Celtic themed stories in Nova Scotia, particularly of the Scottish variety. One story that Fraser relates in her book on Nova Scotia folk belief was told to her by a man whose grandfather swore to its veracity: two men carrying kegs of whiskey home saw the local fairy hill[12] opened and went in, not to be seen again for two years until the hill was seen to open again and some of their neighbours effected a rescue by going in after the two men, who were unaware of how much time had passed, and forced them out (Fraser, 1975). The rescue was aided by the use of some steel placed in the entrance of the fairy hill, which held the space open so the men could safely enter and leave again. This entire story is identical to those found across Celtic speaking cultures but is here situated firmly in Nova Scotian geography.

This excerpt from Fraser's book shows the way that the beliefs were carried over and sometimes held a tinge of surprise that the fairies should be found where they were:

"Mr. Murphy told me of another prank played by the fairies on the farm adjoining his grandfather's lot at Low Point. A man from the old country went out reaping one day in a field of this farm, when, lo and behold! he perceived that all the stooks previously made had been turned upside down. "I didn't think we had any of the 'little people' in this part of the world." he declared in his astonishment." (Fraser, 1975).

Stories of fairies have been passed down in families in Cape Breton, holding to the older view of fairies as potentially dangerous, likely to steal humans or take the essence from milk and to avenge any insults against themselves, including humans speaking badly of them (McLarty, 2022). As with the beliefs and stories we find elsewhere this reflects the way these beings were and are understood in Western Europe and shows the way that the folklore was carried over with the populations who held them. This account from the 2010s was recorded by the Fairy Census, pages 154 – 155:

"We were watching the stars on December 21 of 2012 just past midnight when we both saw a woman step out of the woods. The area where we were was basically a large aspen tree of nine trees grown together surrounded by woods. Beautiful place. She had along silver, purple and green gown and looong [sic] hair with seven stars in it. She seemed to be made of light with what might have been a crown on it. She walked from the woods and paused at the tree, looking right at us before walking INTO the tree. Then it was as though the shadows began to close in and something larger descended from the tree – like a big spider. Needless to say we did NOT stick around. We left in a hurry. After that my friend who also saw it had some terrible spree of bad luck which ended when he later returned to the place with a gift and an apology."

Prince Edward Island

One encounter of particular note is discussed by Woodyard and Young in their 2019 article *Three Notes and a Handlist of North American Fairies*, featured in section three *A Trans-Atlantic Fairy Flight*. The story was originally recounted in the Prince Edward Island magazine of 1902, and is itself a retelling of an anecdote shared with the article's author about an event witnessed in the early to mid-1800s. At that time a local man went missing from a large social gathering, with strange evidence in the snow giving the impression that he had been physically carried off into the air; upon his return he was coated in salt and soaking wet and explained that the fairies often plagued him and, on that night, had abducted him and carried him over the ocean to Europe and then back (Woodyard & Young, 2019). The themes present in the story of both the fairies habitually bothering an individual and of them carrying their target off into the air by magical means reflect similar stories found in Ireland and Scotland.

Chapter 3

The United States

When fairies in North America are discussed, it is natural for many to look to Canada, especially Newfoundland, because of the vibrant beliefs there and the array of written material about them, particularly the work of Barbara Rieti. However, while more diffuse, we do find a wide range of fairy encounters and folklore in the United States as well and it is this material that we will be looking at in this chapter.

Just as we find in Canada, we also have place names in the United States that include fairy or fairy related terms, including Hob. Hob is a somewhat more difficult term to parse as it has historically had a range of meanings, including a nickname for Robert or Robin, and in more recent usage has come to be associated with the hearth. In the 16th and 17th centuries it was used as a prefix on goblin, giving us hobgoblin, to indicate a goblin that was less malicious than the usual and this was shortened later to simply Hob[13] (Briggs, 1976). In England hob is found in various areas as a place name, usually combined with hole,[14] with attached folklore. There are at least four instances of place names in the United States which feature the term hob, the oldest of which is found in records from 1651; all of the sites occur in a state which was one of the original 13 colonies (Woodyard & Young, 2019).

Just as we saw in Canada we find a variety of stories of fairy encounters in the United States, encompassing a wide range of named types of fairies as well as the more general. Woodyard and Young explicitly note 88 such encounters recorded across the United States from 1697 through the mid-20th century. These stories can be taken as a whole about fairies generally but can also be viewed more specifically based on exactly what type of being was discussed, which also demonstrates the diversity of folk belief. I will list the encounters by type and number of occurrences here:

Banshee 19
Brownie 1
Changeling 3
Dwarf 3
Fairy 25
Gnome 3
Goblin 2
Hobgoblin 1
Imp 1
Knocker/Tommyknocker 14
Leprechaun 2
Pixies 3
Uncertain/nonspecific type 7
Abduction by fairies 2
Elfshot 1
Fairy music 2

This is, of course, only one source for fairy stories in the United States and I would like to turn here to another work by Dr Simon Young, the Fairy Census. This text can be found free online and represents anecdotal accounts of fairies across, roughly the last 60 years, including sightings in the US. As important as I think it is in this present work to document historic or older fairy encounters and beliefs, it is also important to show the continuity of these beliefs and their continued occurrence into the 21st century. The Fairy Census notes 210[15] encounters in the US between the 1970s and 2010s, ranging from banshee experiences to fairy dogs, from glowing orbs of light to fairy music. These accounts are found in 42[16] of the 50 states, with about a dozen given by region (New England or Pacific northwest) or simply as 'US'.

Below I'm going to offer some specific examples from two US regions that tend to have a higher amount of preserved fairy folklore followed by a collection of stories from around the US.

New England

Local folklore in New England is not devoid of fairies, and it's clear that people there both presently and in past centuries believed that these beings were around. In 1878 the Hartford Courant, in Connecticut, ran a letter written by someone who claimed that a friend's son saw 'wood-nymphs' which the child labelled goblins; these beings went unseen by others but the child, who was seven years old, was adamant that they existed and interacted with him (Woodyard, 2023).

I know of one story of a man who saw fairies in Connecticut in the late 19th century;[17] he ran a small store in the west part of the state and had a reputation among the local people for seeing and speaking to the Gentry. One day he disappeared, and no one ever found out where he had gone or why, but there were those who said the fairies had taken him. Some local folklore also paints the man as a fairy himself (Woodyard & Young, 2019).

On a more modern note, there is also the story of the Little People's Village in Middlebury Connecticut, a village of tiny houses. Built about 100 years ago as part of an amusement park attraction (originally called the Fairy Village) it fell into ruin after shutting down and is now the focal point of local folklore which says the fairies inhabit it and can sometimes be heard by visitors. The place is claimed as a centre of negative energy and the fairies there are said to cause insanity to those who linger too long or offend them. There is one particular object called the "fairy's throne" and people say if you sit on it you will go mad.

Across the 19th century there were at least four accounts of fairies or fairy-like beings, ranging from dwarves to a hobgoblin as well as the typical fairies, noted in Connecticut. For example, author and abolitionist Harriet Beecher Stowe, as a child in Litchfield, claimed to have seen a dwarf accompanied by a woman wearing white (Woodyard & Young, 2019).

Marblehead Massachusetts featured in an 1894 Folk-lore journal article about local belief in fairies and pixies. The fairies, clearly described through a Victorian lens, were "*good natured little creatures...who were uniformly sweet natured*" and tiny enough to hide beneath flowers; to see one was to ensure good luck throughout a person's life as well as their children's lives (Farmer, 1894, p 252). This idea of fairies as entirely benevolent came into vogue during the 19th century both in the US as well as England, as did the idea that fairies were tiny, in contrast to the human-sized ones more commonly found across folk belief in Ireland, Scotland, and Wales. As with older European folklore they were said to live underground in "*palaces built of gold and silver ornamented with pearls and precious gems*" and to appear at night to dance, leaving behind fairy rings which unlike their transatlantic cousins were seen not in mushroom circles or grass but in lichen and moss (Farmer, 1894, p 252). In contrast the pixies found in the article are closer to their Welsh counterparts, without the Victorian veneer, being described as malevolent and prone to misleading people which the article terms being "*pixilated*" and the remedy is, as in Europe, to turn an item of clothing inside out; the article's author notes that she had talked with a woman who had been pixy led some 60 years prior and escaped by turning her cloak inside out (Farmer, 1894). While this was written in the later part of the 1800s the folk beliefs in the article are positioned as communal and existing across the author's lifetime, continued both in stories told by older community members and in the avid and active belief of local children.

In New York, in 1865, there was a case of an alleged changeling, a toddler who was murdered by his mother because she believed he had been switched for a fairy child. Woodyard and Young reprinted the full newspaper article in *'Three Notes and a Handlist of Fairies in America'*; the article recounts a coroner's inquest against an Irish immigrant who had badly burned her son as part of a test to see if he was really her own child or not (Woodyard & Young, 2019). The child had died a week after being burned and the mother was subsequently committed to an asylum.[18] While extremely grim, this case demonstrates that belief in fairies had been brought over by the woman and was still strong enough to motivate her actions.

Appalachia & the Ozarks

Appalachian culture in the United States was formed by a confluence of influences, including English, Indigenous, Scottish and Scots-Irish.[19] The Scottish and Scots-Irish influence is notable for our purposes here as it created a strong connection between Appalachian folk belief and Western European folk belief, albeit through a unique lens. This influence is perhaps best displayed through the persistent beliefs around fairies which often mirror or draw from existing Irish and Scottish beliefs, sometimes modified with the incorporation of indigenous, particularly Cherokee, beliefs.

Stories can be found across the Appalachian region that include a variety of beings found in European folklore from fairies[20] to the Will'o'the'Wisp. The term 'little people' is commonly used, tying into the similar Cherokee concept of the Yunwi Tsunsdi (little people) and sometimes blurring the folklore between the two. These stories are passed orally, as most of this folk belief is, and while we can make some general statements about it there are variations based on region and even family that add a lot of nuances to each concept (Weston, 2021). The little people, as with their European counterparts, are said to look fairly human and to favour older styles of clothing; they are also believed to be small but able to change their shapes and to take on animal forms (Weston, 2021). Many of the stories we find of little people encounters in these areas are very similar to Irish and Scottish folklore, with a person who helps a fairy in need being rewarded while those who insult or offend them are punished. Unlike European folklore where even seeing the fairies can be risky, in Ozark folklore seeing them, usually in the woods going about their own business, is generally harmless for the human (Weston, 2021).

Brandon Weston in his article *Fairy Faith in the Ozarks* describes several anecdotal accounts that were shared with him. In one a witness described seeing one of the little people milking a groundhog, which is reminiscent of Scottish folklore where wild deer are said to be the fairies' cows. In another account, a woman whose father had been cursed by the little people for blocking a spring during construction was only able to remove the curse by restoring it to its original state. This is in line with a range of European folklore where fairies punished those who despoiled their places or fouled their water sources. Weston also relates a story of a woman who was a folk healer, who claimed to have gotten her skill from the little people after winning a contest of black raspberry picking; her power came with the warning that she would lose it should she ever again eat a black raspberry. This harkens back to a mythic theme in which a person has a special gift or ability but their power or their life is tied into a prohibition not to eat a certain animal. Cu Chulainn and his prohibition about eating dog meat is one example as is Conaire and his prohibition against eating birds. In myths when this prohibition is violated it usually results in the death of the person after they lose all their luck, although in the Appalachian case she would only lose her healing power.

Across the US

An 1896 account from Indiana describes multiple encounters various people had with an unidentified spirit, perhaps a ghost but also possibly a fairy, which would appear on a bridge as a white form or object that rolled or walked across the bridge before disappearing. Chris Woodyard suggests that this may be a kind of boggart[21] as its actions and description fit into wider boggart-lore, and also compares it to a modern account from Dublin (Ireland) of a púca which appeared in a similar rolling white shape (Woodyard, 2023).

Ohio also has several older fairy accounts recorded in newspapers,[22] which relay stories of fairy encounters largely for entertainment. Perhaps the best article headline ever written is attached to one of these stories, from 1911 in Cleveland: *"FLITTING FAIRIES IN WET TREES DRIVE COACHMAN TO FEED MAGIC TORMENTORS: Airy Queens Wreak Vengeance on Man Whose Anger Interrupts Their Play With Little Girls in Park at Dusk."*. In the article it is explained that the coachman, a man named Oliver Sullivan, had disturbed a girl in the park who angrily accused him of making her fairy friends disappear and, when he spoke to her harshly, cursed him saying '*I hope you have trouble*', after which he had a string of bad luck which prompted him to start putting milk, bread, and cheese out as an offering to the fairies to appease their anger (Woodyard, 2023). Milk and bread are common offerings to fairies across western European folklore, and while cheese is less common as a dairy product it is loosely in line with older beliefs that dairy was particularly appreciated by the Good Folk.

There is a 1917 story from Colorado which describes a banshee like being, which wailed and cried and was seen as a large figure wrapped in a white cloth (Woodyard, 2023). It is perhaps interesting to note that the banshee (bean sidhe) seems to be the most common specific fairy being that has carried over to the Americas and survived into modern folklore appearing 19 times in the US section of the Fairy Census, as well in several accounts in Chapter 6 of modern experiences.[23] There may be something more enduring to this particular folklore in part because it is very explicitly tied to family lines and is passed on as a story within families.

One of the most interesting 19th century accounts found in the US comes from Dubuque Iowa, appearing in print in 1886. According to the story, which is reprinted by Chris Woodyard on her website, Haunted Ohio. A young woman who still lived with her father was *"afflicted with a strange malady"* which eventually caused the father to consult a priest; after leaving the priest the young woman declared that he had not helped her and that she would be taken by the fairies a year later. The following year the young woman did disappear, and her father was subsequently accused of her murder and a year later the young woman returned as suddenly as she'd disappeared, claiming she'd been travelling invisibly with the fairies but had been sent back when they became aware of the charges against her father. She was seen by many people and remained for several days before announcing that the fairies had returned to take her back with them. Her sister *"saw two queer-looking beings resembling men dressed in antiquated black costumes"* who the young woman left with; halfway down the block the trio disappeared and the young woman wasn't seen again (Woodyard, 2023).

While not directly related to the topic at hand there is a belief in the Pennsylvania Deitsch communities that some spirits from Germany exist in North America as well. A story found in that community, called the Bauer's Tale, relates how a woman made a deal with the fairies – on the advice of a witch – to give them the cream from her best cow in exchange for help around the farm. This continued after her death although her son was ignorant of the agreement; the fairies simply took the cream and did the work. However, this system was disrupted when a group of Shawnee raided the farm and took all the milk that had been collected that day, including what was the fairies due. The woman's son woke the next day to find the farm work undone and the farm itself barren and it remained so until he consulted the witch and made amends with the fairies by offering double the usual cream. The story also claims those who stole the milk were cursed by the fairies for the action (Schreiwer, 2014).

Chapter 4

Mexico

A fair argument can be made that the European folk beliefs found in Mexico are not Celtic in origin but rather Spanish, however, I would feel remiss in not including the entirety of North America in this text and there is also an argument to be made for a wider shared belief in fairies and elves across western Europe and for Celtic influence in Iberia (modern Navara and Aragon) and Galicia. That said I am presenting this information without trying to argue for or against the cultural influences that may have shaped them, but rather to offer the most balanced and complete possible view of the subject for readers. I also want to note that my research in this particular area is not strong, as I am not a fluent Spanish speaker and have to rely on translated or English language sources.

There seem to be three main terms in Mexico that are generally given as fairy or elf in English; these terms reflect a blending of European and North American concepts.

Duendes – Often translated as elves, Rafael Castro in his book *Chicano Folklore* defines Duende as gnome or goblin-like beings, small and prone to playing tricks on people. They can be helpful especially around farms but can also be disruptive and were noted to follow families who moved to get away from them (Castro, 2001). In some Mexican folklore it's said that Duende will mark a person over the course of several nights then take the person, who will not be seen again (Lopez, 2022). The term, which is widespread across Mexico, Central and South America and can even be found (as dwende) in the Philippines, spread to these places via Spanish colonialism. Originating in medieval and early modern Europe the concept seemed to initially indicate a spirit haunting a house and later as a general term for what we might label fairies, but has taken on different layers across the range of places where the belief is found today (Alexander, 2023).

Pichilingis – An indigenous Aztec term which Castro gives in English as elf, leprechaun, and goblin and which he suggests represents an indigenous equivalent of the Duende (Castro, 2001). There appears to be considerable overlap between the two beings who are both described as childlike and child sized and prone to mischievous tricks.

Chaneques – Beings from Nahuatl folklore that overlap with the Duendes are Chaneques. These are not beings from European folklore but are indigenous to Mexico, however, the beliefs around them are similar to European ones. Chaneques are child-sized beings who protect wild places, who can be helpful or dangerous to humans, and who sometimes steal things from people; turning one's clothes inside out protects against them (México Desconocido, 2023).

This description collected by the USC digital folklore archives describes Duendes, the confusion around them, and some beliefs connected to them:

> *"So, there are these things called duendes, which are like gnomes and I guess they're, like, cousins or something, they're, like, related to leprechauns, essentially. And they're popular, or known about, not just in Mexico, but also in, like, Central America, like El Salvador, or, um, in other parts of South America. And, um, apparently, from what I understand is, these, like, leprechaun-like creatures, these gnomes, they can, they like–, they choose a house or something and, um, when they choose a house, um, like, they'll,*

like, try and, like, live in the house, but you can't really see them, I don't know, like, adults can't really see them, I guess. But if you do see it, you have to give it food, um, because if you don't give it food, it will, like, play pranks on you for the rest of your life." (Lavelle, 2013).

The fairy census offers two accounts from Mexico. The first occurred in the 2010's from a woman who saw two fairies in a rose garden:

"One was small didn't look like it was clothed and either had something on its head, maybe blonde hair. The other was just this face looking at me through some leaves." (Young, 2018, p 384).

The second was during the same period, but rather than a single encounter was a man who described himself as a fairy investigator who had taken thousands of pictures of fairies, who he understood to be nature spirits that could change shape (Young, 2018). An online article by Cheniliz Lopez relates three stories of a family's interactions with Duende, or 'elves'; in the first the author describes her cousin, as a child, hearing unnerving childlike laughter, in the second a family story that claims the Duende were responsible for her grandmother's disappearance, and finally a story from her aunt's childhood where she had heard and seen two Duende who tried to lure her and her sister into the woods (Lopez, 2022).

Chapter 5

Popculture Fairies in North America

Up until this point we have largely been looking at historic accounts of fairies that are recorded between the mid-17th and mid-20th centuries; these accounts are most strongly in line with the folklore that was and still is found in the Celtic language speaking cultures of Europe and form a basis to support the idea that Celtic fairies exist outside the traditionally Celtic countries. In this chapter I am going to turn my attention to encounters recorded since 1950, but before we delve into that a few points must be made about the changing nature of fairy encounters across the last 70 years and the influences on these changes. While we still use the term fairy and we still generally associate these beings with Celtic language speaking cultures, the folklore in North America has diverged, in some cases significantly, from older material.

There is no question that people have recounted encounters with beings either explicitly described as Celtic fairies or which fit that description in the 20th and 21st centuries in North America, meaning that these beliefs are not artifacts of the past but active today. A good source for these accounts is Part 2 of the Fairy Census,[24] a work produced by the Fairy Investigation Society which spent several years recording anecdotal material sent in by people around the world and has offered it free to the public. What this shows us is that belief in fairies continues across a range of locations and also that there are still people who believe that fairies, of various sorts, can be found outside the Celtic language speaking cultures. However, studying these sources also shows us the way that popular culture impacts belief in and understanding of these beings, and reshapes people's expectations of encounters. The fairies, hobs, and elves of historic American folklore are not identical to the fairies found in accounts today, although arguably the belief in them shares a common root.

Modern popculture fairies have been largely shaped by three main factors: Theosophy, the Victorians, and modern fiction. We will discuss each of these separately, as its vital to understand the ways that these factors have created a new understanding of fairies which uses the terminology of the older folklore and that specific to Celtic cultures. It is these three influences that have given us modern fairy folklore in North America that is almost antithetical to Celtic folklore, but which uses the same terms and loose concepts. It is also important to note that the popculture view is almost always framed through the lens of Celtic cultures, as well as English fairy beliefs, without any acknowledgement of the differences; the beliefs have seemingly existed continuously despite having been very radically redefined across the last hundred years, so much so that the fairies of North American popculture wouldn't necessarily be recognized as fairies elsewhere – nonetheless we will be treating them as fairies in deference to the beliefs of the people who call them such.

First, we need to outline clearly the profound influence that Theosophy has had on fairy belief over the last 130 years. Although not as well known today as it may have been in the late 19th and early 20th century, Theosophy has had a profound impact on how some people engage with fairies and has shaped the wider popculture understanding of these beings in significant ways.

A main influence on the neopagan view of fairies, which is rarely acknowledged, is theosophy and more particularly the writings of Helena Blavatsky. Blavatsky herself is a controversial figure, accused of rampant plagiarism by her contemporaries and criticized today for her theories on race expressed in *The Secret Doctrine*; that said her influence on neopaganism and western witchcraft traditions is profound if often ignored. In particular Blavatsky reimagined who and what fairies were and forwarded that in her writing; her ideas were picked up by occultists of her time, including WB Yeats, and seeped into esoteric thought on the subject. So, let us explore that.

To begin, we must quickly establish the understanding of fairies in folklore. What we find across the breadth of western European material are beings who can be intangible or physical at will, who are intrinsically connected to humanity in ways that are both helpful and predatory, and who exist both in and outside of the human world. These are beings in some cases who were formerly human and who steal living humans without compunction and beings who were once Gods. They must be warded against and also propitiated to stay on good terms and avoid harm.

We must digress here for a space to discuss Paracelsus, because his views are foundational for later ideas of fairies as elementals, but are often misunderstood. A common defence of the idea of fairies as elementals that I often see is the claim that it was actually the 15th/16th century Paracelsus who originated this idea and that it is therefore genuinely historic and true to older European folklore. However, its slightly more complicated than that, and the modern understanding that we have has been refined and influenced by other ideas, including those of theosophy.

The view Paracelsus was advocating wasn't based in the four (or five) element system or in a strict division of fairies into four groups. Rather he was discussing the nature of all things as relating to different elements – he mentions seven – based on what they seem most connected to in his opinion. It is worth noting as well that initially he assigns sylphs to the earth, along with four other types of beings, 'sylvani' to air, and associates nymphs – not undine – with water:

"So it is to be known also further that the spirits are many, and they are each one differently than the other. For there are spiritus coelestes, spiritus infernales, spiritus humani, spiritus ignis, spiritus aëris, spiritus aquae, spiritus terrae, etc.. And the spiritus coelestes [spirits of heaven] are the angels and the best spirits, the spiritus infernales [spirits of Hell] are the devils, the spiritus humani [human spirits] are the dead human spirits, the spiritus ignis [spirits of fire] are the salamanders, the spiritus of the air are the sylvani, the spiritus aquatici [spirits of water] are the nymphs, the spiritus terrae [spirits of earth] are called the sylphs, pygmies, Schrötlein, Büzlein, and mountain men."
– Paracelsus, Tractatus IV

Later in writing *Ex Libro de Nymphis, Sylvanis, Pygmaeis, Salamandris, et Caetebus Spiritus* (the book of nymphs, sylvanis, pygmies, salamanders, and other spirits) he would expand these groups and did include undine with water and gnomes with earth. However, he didn't limit these beings to single elements, instead listing three elements that each needed, one that they existed in and two others that they were nourished by (Willard, 2020). His elementals then were more complex and nuanced than the modern versions, and were also part of a complex system through which they might reproduce with a human to create a spirit with a soul or with other elemental beings to create monsters which included by his reckoning dwarves, giants, and mermaids. He also understood these beings as having a middle nature between the physical and non-physical, and being inherently good beings who were open to evil influences but sought God and longed for souls (Willard, 2020). Paracelsus also, rather ironically to us perhaps, did not use the names he chose for these beings by choice but rather because he felt they were recognizable (despite appearing to be the source for sylph and gnome) and instead, as Willard discusses more eloquently than I can here, preferred to call them people and emphasize their likeness to humans.[25]

In Blavatsky's view, however, we see none of the folkloric fairy and only a shadow of Paracelsus' ideas. We find fairies – interchangeably called elementals and nature spirits – described as lesser beings who seek to evolve upwards into human souls and who are incapable of physical form or of higher intelligence:

"They are the Soul of the elements, the capricious forces in Nature, acting under one immutable Law, inherent in these Centres of Force, with undeveloped consciousness and bodies of plastic mold, which can be shaped according to the conscious or unconscious will of the human being who puts himself in rapport with them ... These beings have never been, but will in myriads of ages hence, be evolved into men. They belong to the three lower kingdoms ... Elementals, as said already, have no form, and in trying to describe what they are, it is better to say that they are 'centers of force' having instinctive desires, but no consciousness, as we understand it. Hence their acts may be good or bad indifferently." (Blavatsky, 1893).

In modern theosophy all fairies, under any name, are lumped into the general categories of elemental or nature spirit (Theosophy World, 2023). It is broadly understood that all named types of folkloric beings are actually cultural interpretations of specific categories of elementals/nature spirits. These beings are also more strictly limited to their single element and categorized into one of three kingdoms which all seek to evolve into mineral, seen as a transition point into higher evolution which leads eventually to human incarnation (Theosophy World, 2023). While Paracelsus described these various spirits as very humanoid and capable of interacting with and even reproducing with humans, Theosophy sees them as entirely intangible, shaped or given appearance by human assumptions or projections, and as less intelligent and more primitive than humans. They are, from this view, nature embodied in spirit and exist in a world where humans are the ultimate goal of spiritual evolution, a state which all 'lesser' spirits seek to achieve by working their way up a hierarchy of incarnation, from the elemental state into form then into humanity.

Another key aspect which is paraphrased by the Theosophy World website is that fairies/elementals are *"neither individualized like human beings nor even yet entered on the way to such individualization, as animals and plants have been"*. Or in other words, elementals in this view are a collective consciousness, an expression of a natural force, rather than a unique or individual being. This is an aspect of the lower evolution of these spirits compared to humans, that they exist in a primitive state and are not conscious or self-aware in a way that humans understand. This is also reflected in the idea that these beings lack any form of their own and are only given form by the humans they interact with. They are understood to be immoral or amoral in that they lack the cognitive ability to make moral judgements and instead act by 'natural law' (Theosophy World, 2023). This is, of course, sharply in contrast to Paracelsus' idea of elementals as inherently good but capable of being misled into evil, as it positions them as incapable of any moral understanding or judgment.

So, what are the key points that popular culture has taken from Blavatsky that are at odds with folklore?

Fairies as incorporeal – A common idea seen in modern views that is rooted in Blavatsky but not found elsewhere is that fairies are incapable of being tangible or corporeal.

Fairies are beneath humans – Blavatsky placed fairies as less evolved souls and simple primitive spirits. While there are corners of neopaganism who view fairies as evolved guides there are also many who see fairies as animalistic and easily controlled by humans or existing in a hierarchy beneath humans.

Fairies as nature spirits – While this is concurrent with Victorian imagery it was also a point that Blavatsky specifically wrote about, tying fairies intrinsically to the human natural world and particularly plants and minerals. In this view, fairies are limited to and defined by the human natural world.

Fairies as elementals – Widely popular now and seen even outside neopaganism, is the Blavatsky idea of fairies as elemental spirits. This view generally removes the nuanced belief about fairies and reduces them to simple expressions of the qualities of an element. While claiming to be based on Paracelsus, this view is often more strongly informed by Blavatsky.

Fairies require human input to express forms – I have seen this in multiple contexts now, the idea that fairies are formless unless and until given form through interaction with a human. Put another way, humans see what they expect when encountering a fairy because they shape themselves to the human's expectation.

Fairies seek human incarnation – while we have a plethora of material, including Paracelsus, which discuss the fairies desire for souls and Christian salvation it seems to be an effect of Theosophy to believe that fairies desire or seek physical form in a human body.[26] This seems to have blended into some neopagan/witchcraft ideas around reincarnation and the afterlife to give us a belief in witches as fairy souls incarnate in human bodies or humans being corporeal fairies who return to Fairy after death.

We do find stories, such as that of Melusine, that discuss a fairy reproducing with a human so that their offspring will have a soul, but that is a rather different concept.

Fairies as simple or childlike spirits – an outgrowth of Blavatsky's ideas of fairies/elementals as less evolved and less intelligent spirits, possibly blended with the Victorian infantilization of fairies, seems to be the idea of fairies as childlike spirits.

It should be understood that these ideas often work together or intertwine in modern thought, sometimes independent of other influences, sometimes closely tied to related Victorian or new age beliefs, and sometimes woven into older folk material to create a new concept. If your understanding of fairies involves their being less than human, incapable of corporeal form, as childlike spirits, as beings who are bound to the natural world or as elemental beings embodying natural forces then you are being influenced by theosophical thought and its followers in occult and pagan philosophy.

Victorians are the second factor which has impacted modern understandings of fairies, in conjunction with Theosophy. This effect is most noticeable in how fairies are physically described or depicted and from that how people now assume they will appear. Let's look at two of the main aspects

Fairies with wings – One of the most fascinating popculture impacts on fairies is undoubtedly their now almost ubiquitous portrayal with wings. Fairies in older folklore and in Western Europe were understood as being able to fly via magical means and were not described with wings, in fact generally looked fairly human. This has changed significantly in modern North American accounts where there is now a presumption that fairies are inherently winged and where wings often featured in descriptions from anecdotes, such as this one:

"More than one fairy approached me, flitted about and tried to get me to follow them deeper into the woods. They looked exactly like little human beings with wings."

Or this one:

"At first I thought it was just a very pretty colorful butterfly flitting around me but the body was definitely not that of a butterfly. The body was that of a very beautiful lady." (Young, 2018, p 207, p 295).

The idea of fairies with wings gained great popularity across the Victorian era in art and artists started depicting fairies with wings. This may have been meant as a visual cue to viewers to make it clear the subject of the art were fairies or it may have represented a merging of the older understanding of fairies with the burgeoning idea of these beings as embodiments of nature and natural things, a concept which crystalized in the late 19th century with theosophies rewriting of fairies into elementals and nature spirits. Initially, however, the change from non-winged fairies to winged wasn't decisive, and we see artists using both styles of imagery. For example, Francis Danby created two paintings themed around Shakespeare the first from 1832 'Scene From a Midsummer Night's Dream' shows Oberon and Titania with wings while the second 'Oberon and Titania' from 1837 does not. Through the 1870's we can find examples of fairies both with and without wings in art. By the 1880s, however, the wings dominate and can be found in all, or nearly all, artistic depictions of these beings. These wings are most often butterfly wings, occasionally more general insect wings, and range from small to larger than the figure itself. We also begin to see these visual cues used to gender these beings with female winged fairies and male elves with pointed ears, although there is some crossover between the two types of imagery.

It is also at this point that Theosophy begins, both taking the visual imagery of fairies found in art and also creating – or solidifying – the idea that fairies are spirits of the natural human world who are less than and dependent on humans. The combination of these two factors, Victorian cultural depictions and Theosophical descriptions, would combine to entirely rewrite the popular culture understanding of fairies in ways that are still affecting us today. By the late Victorian era we find the idea of winged fairies, as shown in art, starting to crossover into fiction, and during the Edwardian period and first world war the wider cultural concept of fairies as small, winged, and connected to the natural world becomes nearly ubiquitous in English and American culture so that by the late 20th century people start to describe personal encounters with small winged fairies.

Fairies with pointed ears[27] – When we look at descriptions of fairies, under different names, from folklore we generally find their human-like appearance being emphasized. As Andrew Lang says:

"There seems little in the characteristics of these fairies of romance to distinguish them from human beings, except their supernatural knowledge and power." (Wimberly, 1965).

Yeats, in the late 19th century relates this description of a Fairy woman given to him by a woman in Ulster:

"She was like a woman about thirty, brown-haired and round in the face. She was like Miss Betty, your grandmother's sister, and Betty was like none of the rest, not like your grandmother, nor any of them. She was round and fresh in the face..." (Yeats, 1902).

In all of these examples and others across folklore we see fairy people being described without pointed ears and notably with a very human-like appearance, usually the only indication of their Otherworldly nature comes through their actions, demeanour, an energy or feeling around them, or a perception people have of them as such.

The concept of elves and fairies with pointed ears in Western culture is likely rooted in Christian demonic imagery. This is because Christianity, in seeking to explain the existence of elves and fairies, fit them into the cosmology as a type of demon or fallen angel, which logically led to people imagining demonic characteristics onto fairies. As far back as 1320 we can find depictions of demons with pointed ears, usually along with other physical deformities, especially animalistic features (Bovey, 2006). These pointed ears and horrific appearances are in sharp contrast to the way that angelic and divine beings are depicted, emphasizing through physical depiction the hellish nature of these demonic beings. Whereas the saved souls and angels are emphatically human, the demons are just as emphatically inhuman with their obvious animal features, including their ears. This is likely an intentional device to make the demons unappealing and frightening, in opposition to the relatable human-like angels. In folklore we also often see fairies described with animal features, including tails or webbed feet, as well as physical deformities like hollow backs; although fairies are just as often described as beautiful as they are grotesque. Because Christianity chose to depict demons in the way that it did and because they explained fairies in their cosmology as a type of demon or fallen angel, and because fairylore itself described fairies as having physical features that could fit the later Christian descriptions of demons there was a certain inevitability in the artistic depictions of the two types of beings blending together.

Looking further back, though, we see that there were some beings in Greek and Roman mythology that did have animalistic features and potentially pointed ears, including beings like satyrs, which were described with ears that could be either donkey like or goat like in shape, and in artwork this is easily perceived as pointed (Atsma, 2017). In the King James version of the Bible there are references to satyrs,[28] which may be a mistranslation of the Hebrew word for a type of spirit (Jackson, 2017). Even though a mistranslation is likely in that case it speaks to a cultural perception that related satyrs to demons. The word in question that is being given as satyr is sa'im which may be a corruption of the Hebrew seirim. In Old Testament demonology the seirim was a being that blended the attributes of a goat and a demon, based perhaps on the practice of representing a demon by a symbolic animal with similar attributes (Rodriguez, 2017). It is likely that the classical depictions of satyrs influenced that later Christian depictions of demons.

Early depictions of elves and fairies in artwork show them in line with folklore depictions, that is mostly human like in appearance although they may be either beautiful or ugly and were sometimes shown as very small. As we enter into the Victorian era, we begin to see elves and fairies shown with pointed ears, probably based on popular imagery of Puck which in turn drew on demonic imagery that was drawing on the depictions of satyrs (Wright, 2009). Puck was a popular folkloric figure that had long blended fairylore and demonology, understood as a type of fairy, individual being, and also a name for the Devil (Wright, 2009). This blurring of fairylore and Christian cosmology was fertile ground for artwork and laid the foundation for a wider understanding of fairies through this lens; the artists of the Victorian era slowly refined the concept so that what began as pointed ears only on the wildest of fey beings eventually spread to pointed ears even on the delicate winged nature sprites. By the 19th century artists began depicting elves and fairies with pointed ears almost exclusively. By the 20th century we see these descriptions entering written media with both prose and poetry describing elves and fairies with pointed ears. Even Tolkien tentatively described his Hobbits with slightly pointed ears and his Elves, at one time, with pointed or leaf shaped ears[29] (Dunkerson, 2017). The concept has now become ubiquitous, spreading throughout popculture and into folklore, so that it is simply taken as a given that elves and fairies have pointed ears. Pointed ears became a quick way to signal to a viewer that the subject of a piece wasn't human even if they seemed so in all other ways, or in other cases to emphasize their inhuman nature.

Modern fiction across the last 30 or so years has also played a role in redefining the fairy of popculture. This includes both movies and TV as well as books, which work to give a new narrative understanding of fairies and act to fill in gaps in knowledge or details to those who are disconnected from older folk beliefs. Mass media has stepped into the place of the oral storyteller and filled the gap left for people who have no other sources for such information. The strongest effect this has had to date has been a slow reshaping, particularly among neopagans and witches, of the idea of fairies as dangerous into a view wherein the human becomes a kind of main character in their own story with all the expected plot armour such a character would have in a story. There has also been a notable reshaping of the dangerous beings of the Scottish Unseelie court into friendly allies and even love interests. Finally, fiction is also informing how people understand the social structure of fairies and particularly who they believe rules as a king or queen of these beings. When I inquired on social media the answers I received were largely drawing from the works of Holly Black, Jim Butcher, and Laurel K Hamilton, and these three were also the main sources that people suggested for those interested in learning more about fairies. In this way modern fiction, particularly urban fantasy, has filled the niche of the oral stories of yesterday and is creating an amalgam of beliefs that blend older folklore, fiction, and imagination.

One final modern aspect of fairies I'd like to touch in is the idea of fairies as formless balls of light. In older folklore fairies are generally described as physical, tangible beings who have a clear form, whether that form is human-like or animal-like or changing between both. However, as we move into the 20th century, we find the idea of physical fairies eroding in popculture to be replaced by the concept of fairies as disembodied and formless. This may perhaps be traced back to the emergence of theosophy which we've previously discussed or possibly the stage depiction of Tinkerbell in the play *Peter Pan* as a glowing light, or, of course, both of these things together. *Peter Pan's* Tinkerbell wasn't portrayed by an actor, as in past plays which had fairy characters, but was shown only as a small flickering light. This was, at the time, a cutting-edge special effect achieved by reflecting light off a mirror and directing it across the stage by adjusting the mirror's direction. As we move into the 20th century anecdotal accounts which feature fairies as formless lights or orbs have become common with this example, from the Fairy Census, being typical:

"...*little floating lights dancing in the street on my cul-de-sac. They were too bright to make out, but I'm pretty sure they were fairies.*" (Young, 2018, p320)

These fairies may not reflect the older folk beliefs of the source cultures, tending to lean into the wider popular culture beliefs that grew out of the older ones, but they do still show the power and persistence of belief. They are also, despite their popculture roots, most often labelled or understood as Celtic cultural fairies and while this may not be true it is an aspect of the folk belief around them and must be taken into account when considering modern folklore about them.

Chapter 6

Contemporary Experiences

Now that we've looked at the range of older evidence to show that the belief in fairies in North America has been around for more or less as long as Europeans have been there, I'd like to explore some modern accounts. These represent personal experiences that were relayed to me after I asked for people who had encountered Celtic fairies in North America to share their stories, and are being presented here, largely, in the words of the person who had the experience. I am not editing these stories nor providing any commentary, but am simply presenting them to the reader to be taken as they are.

This is in no way an exhaustive study of modern beliefs and represents a small sample size, largely within the modern neopagan community, but I believe that it does show the way these beliefs are still active in North America as part of a changing but continuous thread of folk belief.

Queen of Elphame

"Although I don't have a close dynamic with her, I respect and have interacted with the Scottish Queen of Elphame. I've given her offerings at a hawthorn tree in a graveyard in the Midwest United States, and while that specific tree didn't feel like it was "hers," nor aligned to her, per se, the tree nonetheless allowed for an appropriate place to offer and to boost the signal to connect with her.

In one of the trance journeys I've had where I communicated with her, she was human-shaped and sized, standing outside a forest clearing with an entire procession of people with her, some of whom were holding the train of her dress/cloak. She was wearing a dark green gown and cloak. The cloak appeared to be lined on the inside with some kind of big game cat fur, possibly snow leopard. I was kneeling in front of her the whole time, and she allowed me to kiss her hand.

In another trance experience, I visited her court and perceived time to be moving extremely quickly as if I was inside a movie that was getting fast-forwarded, to the degree that as she asked me questions, I had no time to carefully consider my answers but instead felt like I had to respond from pure impulse and, if I said something I felt I shouldn't have said, my only chance to correct it was by adding more words onto the sentence to change the meaning, rather than being able to correct myself or prevent missteps in the first place. It was terrifying, energizing, and instructive. I often perceive her as an excellent educator. She's treated me with patience and seems willing to offer lessons that test and expand my magical skills, though I have often felt nervous when interacting directly." -Bat Collazo

An Púca/the Puca/the Puck/Robin Goodfellow

"As is fitting for An Púca, trying to understand this name/category/identity has been difficult for me to wrap my head around and even more confusing to research properly. There's An Púca or the Puca (singular individual, heavy emphasis on the "the" article), multiple other different individual people of various kinds all being called the Puca, púcaí and pookas and pucks as plural, the Puck, and an absurd number of variations. "Hey, did you see the puca over there?" has a completely different connotation than, "Hey, did you see The Puca over there?" All I can say with some small degree of temporary confidence, thanks to personal experience and thanks to the work of Irish scholar Deasún Breatnach, is that, in my opinion, the Puca as a solitary supernatural entity in Irish folklore is often (though not always) the same individual as the Puck, Robin Goodfellow, and several other names, a fairy-related being who travels throughout various parts of the world and has mysterious origins. (A chapbook from 1643 calls him a "vagabond elf" and the theme of world travel and no single, permanent home recurs regularly.) That said, since puca/puck in the plural basically refers to spirits with certain traits, there seem to be many stories using puck-type words that refer to other individual or collective spirits instead. For me, I focus on the person I have an oath to, who is (in part) the overlap of the Venn diagram of the Puca, the Puck, and Robin Goodfellow. He shows up in multiple Celtic cultures at different times, even though he appears in several non-Celtic contexts too.

I have an ongoing relationship with him, rather than just one anecdote. He first startled, intimidated, and intrigued me by introducing himself unexpectedly when I was traveling in the Midwest United States, where I now live. He appeared, the energy in the room completely shifted, and we talked (while I tried not to freak out and did an okay job playing it cool). I only knew what to call him (and eventually how to begin researching him) because he told me that he was Robin Goodfellow – otherwise, with my limited knowledge at the time, I would not have been able to recognize him, I would have only known he was some kind of powerful being. At the time I first met him, I knew next to nothing about fairies.

He's guided me to find some of his different recorded anecdotes in various locations and to learn more about him, but he can also be vague or misleading, which in all fairness I do enjoy despite my frustration. When I asked him outright one day if he was An Púca in Irish folklore, his response was, "Why look so far for what's already near?" (He was in my house during this conversation.) Thanks to my bias as a hard polytheist, and my wariness about the colonial implications of conflating a spiritual being often seen as English with a being from Irish lore, I assumed this Puck had no direct connection to Ireland or the Puca, but he and my research have both since corrected me. Today, I dare not guess where he's from "originally" or confine his history to one region only, though colonization certainly plays a role in how his stories traveled. As far as I can tell, multiple cultures and regions have encountered him, and some anecdotes (in Ireland, England, Cornwall, the USA, etc) are the same guy, hopping between towns, nations, islands, or even continents, whereas other anecdotes are people who share some traits with him being called similar terms. I think these both happen, and it's impossible to empirically confirm which is which. But it is a very fun wild goose chase, and I have intuitive guesses and spiritual gnosis.

When I encounter him, I see him in multiple forms: usually either adult human-sized and human-appearing in a few common forms, or a slightly smaller dark-furred bipedal or quadrupedal creature prone to climbing and squatting on things. He's unclothed in the less human form. When he's in human form it's either naked or sometimes wearing fairly modern clothes, including tailored business suits. I sometimes also see him as a satyr, a black horse, black bear, or black dog, or sometimes other forms. I currently find it difficult to "focus" my gaze on him, regardless of whether I'm getting a brief glimpse in the physical world, or whether in my mind's eye. I know what he looks like to me, but if I try to hold onto that image to draw him or even think about the exact shape of his features, it blurs out. Stylized or abstract drawings seem to work better in my experience of him.

I leave him regular offerings of things like carbs, butter, cream, and other dairy products, honey, alcohol, and occasionally bacon. Early on, I had a knife accident (or "accident" depending on one's interpretation) and bled pretty badly while making a wood carving of him, which I consider an unintentional blood offering, but since then I've gotten a tattoo for him on purpose and will occasionally give him other intentional blood offerings. Though he can be dangerous, I do believe he wants me to be healthy and whole. When I encounter him, we usually just enjoy each other's company in a pretty domestic way, rather than something dramatic happening every time. Sometimes he takes me on magical journeys or we discuss serious topics or I get extremely lost in my own city while listening to his playlist, but more often, we connect doing mundane activities or we talk about everyday things. These everyday things include huge proportions of dirty jokes, which sometimes makes anecdotes difficult to share.

In one dream journey, the Puca took the form of a small black bear, and I found myself riding on his back (no reins or saddle, just holding on for dear life) as he ran and climbed and leapt over the edges of precarious gray cliffs with huge, steep drops below. At one point, these cliffs changed into someone's black granite kitchen countertops and we stopped for him to get an offering of corn in a bowl from one specific human family (a mother and two older teenage children), who were all friendly but strangers to me. He paused to chat with them, then he plunged down with me past the dishwasher and we were traveling through cliffs again. The experience was nerve-wracking but fun, and I trusted him throughout it, even if I didn't fully trust myself to hold on well enough." -Bat Collazo

Jack the Smith/Stingy Jack/Jack-o-the-Lantern

"Speaking of multicultural fairy-adjacent spiritual beings, the practice of carving and decorating with jack-o-lanterns at Halloween in the United States probably wouldn't exist if it weren't for Jack. Especially the Irish Jack blacksmith tales, sometimes called "Stingy Jack," and other related stories of Jack using cleverness to trick the Devil and/or Death with the consequence of perpetually wandering the earth on the "middle path" that is neither "Heaven" nor "Hell," all of which are concepts strongly reminiscent of fairy themes in the post-Christian context. What's also suggestive of the Otherworld is the fact that he sometimes misleads travelers as he wanders, similar to the Will-o-the-Wisp (Jack is said to carry one coal or ember inside his lantern, or a carved turnip/rutabaga, or in later versions, a pumpkin). The Irish Jack the Smith or "Stingy Jack" stories usually portray him as a jaded, cunning older man with alcoholism, in contrast to some of the other Jack stories that tend to focus on an optimistic, innocent youth (such as Hans in Luck in Germany). However, several of the Irish (and Scottish Traveller) versions of Jack-o-the-Lantern simultaneously show Jack as good-hearted and hospitable, even if unapologetically "sinful" by Christian standards and sometimes mean, criminal, or devious, depicting him as a complicated figure, and fittingly for the themes, neither pure nor evil.

I became interested in Jack after collaborating on creative writing for years with my human partner, who is passionate about Jack tales. My first direct, unmediated spiritual experience with Jack was during a day of political anxiety and despair about social injustice. I was feeling a lot of existential dread about US laws, and for whatever reason, Jack reached out to me and started talking to me about DIY abortion drugs. I didn't need them myself, and I didn't go out and start trying to make them, but talking to him reminded me that there are activists out there educating people on how to reduce harm when making and using outlawed medications, and that was really useful for my sense of hope and determination. I began making a music playlist for Jack after that, to improve that connection. I now tend to associate Jack with guidance related to "by hook or by crook" type witchcraft and healthcare. As may be obvious from his associations with blacksmithing, I don't find that iron is problematic for Jack, and I have some protective iron objects I associate with him. For divination with him, I use a deck of playing cards that looks like a pack of cigarettes, and I tend to give him alcohol offerings. I usually see Jack as human-shaped, often appearing about 40 but ranging up to about 70 years old in appearance, and usually wearing simple clothes (denim jeans, plain t-shirt). I carve turnip lanterns seasonally when I can, and I have a year-round jack-o-lantern candle holder for him. I suspect he can lie outright, not just by prevaricating, and he's managed to spark a few actual crises in my life, and I'm nonetheless grateful for his presence in it." -Bat Collazo

Encounter with the Tuatha Dé Danann[30]

"My encounter with the Tuatha De Danann was really something more like an initiation. I was living in the remote Siskiyou Wilderness of Northern California on Blue Ridge Ranch. I had moved there from a nearby commune I had been on for a couple years because I was drawn to the impressive grove of black oaks that dwell on the ridge that overlooks the Trinity Alps. I was a young, naive pagan who knew very little about magick and had been reading anything I could get my hands on. I was alone in my spiritual pursuits because none of the people who lived in those mountains shared my interest in the occult, the faerie faith, or witchcraft. I was practicing things no one should be doing alone. I had been drawn particularly to Victor Anderson's Feri Tradition, but also felt very aligned with the Celtic traditions that I had read about. I was also reading a fair amount of Aleister Crowley's works. In addition to this potentially volatile mix, I was an emotionally broken individual with zero human support to help process what was going on inside me.

At the peak of my loneliness, I decided to reach out to the beings who I felt to be my spiritual teachers, the faerie, who I may or may not have also considered to be synonymous with the Tuatha De Danann. On a full moon, somewhere between March and May of 2001 I decided to do a ritual to ask for their help. With my journal that held shattered dreams and hopes, I went into the grove with a bottle of wine, some backstrap from a deer that we had recently processed (I can't recall if it was the one I had shot or if it was one that had died on a fence we

56

had recently constructed), and some cannabis that had grown on the land. I offered these to a tree that I believed to be a portal to the Otherworld. This tree was unique among the other trees in the grove in that it had a large burl that wrapped around the entire trunk and was about the size of a VW Bug. Beneath the burl was an opening in the trunk that went into the ground. I offered the meat and the herb there to the TDD and spread the entire bottle of wine out on the ground. I don't recall what other invocations I may have made or done, but I remember clutching my journal and crying my heart out asking for help. When my tears were spent, I gathered myself and went to bed in the trailer I was staying in only a couple hundred yards away. When next I awoke, I was back in the grove. My hands had been tied behind my back, and an enormous fire had been lit in the clearing inside the grove. But it was not a natural fire, it flickered in many colors and didn't seem to burn the trees as it licked their branches. There was chanting coming from somewhere and there were beings dancing around in my peripheral vision. I could see that the chanting was coming from a horse. Later I would identify this horse as one of the horses on the ranch that had patiently let me wrap my arms around her and grieve in my broken state days before this event. I was on my knees and could see a few figures towering over me. One of them appeared to be rather regal, though I did not know who they were. Other beings that were there had unusual forms. One had many spikes coming from their back, while another seemed to be some kind of warrior with slicked back hair and a sword at their side but hovered over the ground and did not seem to have feet. Someone was behind me with their arms on my shoulders. This being seemed to have a firm but motherly touch to them. But then this being pulled my hair so that my head tilted back and my mouth was opened. The being that seemed to be the leader among them raised a sword above me and brought the tip into my mouth, cutting an incision in the back of my throat.

Into this cut was planted an acorn. There may have been more to this dream but I don't recall. I woke again to find myself back in my bed in the trailer. This period of my life I commonly had prophetic and powerful dreams with spiritual teachers showing me things or magical happenings, but this experience was by far the most profound. I did not then, nor now consider it just a dream, but an out of body experience.

In my journal I remember writing that they had a very Tolkien-esque feel to them. They were a traveling band of warrior fae who were not of that land and had come because I had been calling to them for some time. Part of why this stands out from any other dreams I had had during this time of my life was the potent shift in my poetry that occurred immediately following this experience. I had been writing some before this, but nothing that I particularly felt was worth sharing. Shortly after this, however, I sat down to write a poem to my father who had recently surprised me by writing a poem about me for my birthday (he was not a very creative person).

The poem I wrote in response, however, ended up being a long, looping, lyrical screed on my relationship and overall distaste for patriarchy. I'm not sure if I ever actually shared it with him. Because of the Crowley influence that was prevalent in my consciousness at the time it contained elements I no longer agree with and a certain manic quality that I associate with his toxic influence. It was, however, the beginning of a writing style that I would continue for years. The style was a very non-traditional, irregular style with a lot of alliteration, rhyme that jumped from place to place, and lines that varied in length. It also contained a lot of subversive elements and anti-establishment, cutting qualities. More importantly, however, that first poem and many others would resonate in my mind for days after writing them and I had gained the ability to memorize large chunks of poetry and recite them. Years later this would come to be expressed in the fire circle tradition I was an active member of before joining Coru. I still retain this ability to memorize poetry well, though my writing has subsided for the time being in lieu of other practices, like playing calls for the gods through the carnyx." -Patrick

Family Banshee & Personal Encounters

"There was a banshee that would call when someone was about to die, I don't think during my time, but everyone had some sense, if not sight, of her. Same on mom's side, with that from both sides. Of my experiences, two stood up that have been told, one after an incident & years later someone kinda explained it, though I think that most of it has all passed now. I was at a friend's house with a full glass of wine on the floor & my friend said these things were around me & called themselves guardians of the fail & I go great, this is my luck, then my glass which I was standing away from fell & might have shattered. We looked at each other & went hmmm. Both practitioners of various things but knew they were trying to communicate with me & not getting it. They didn't want to talk to my friend & I had blocked myself. I did immediately think of an incident when I was about 13 or so & woke up to something sitting on my bed talking to me & I couldn't understand so I said I can tell what you are saying & he (felt male) got up & disappeared, think same thing as wine glass incident. The true lucid dream of romping around next time a pond or lake but beautiful warm day sun out laying around on green grass with a young man my age talking joking & playing (sensual but not sexual per se). He was perfect, gorgeous with blonde hair in curls & blue eyes & told me his name & said to call him if I ever needed help, I never did but thought of him since" -Kathy

Strange Lights

"On January 15th, 2022, I had gone to Deeply Rooted Church in Athens, WI, with my Norse Kindred, Raven Hof, (I'm the token Celt) for Yule. We'd celebrated as you do, with ritual, decorating Yule Logs, making and burning Goat effigies, feasting, drinking, exchanging gifts etc. Sometime around midnight, a couple of my kindred and I decided to take a walk in the snow through the woods. We visited our ancestor altar near the hemlock Grove and started back to the cabin. One of us decided to head back and the three of us left, turned to walk around in the moonlit snow a bit longer, wanting to explore areas we hadn't before. The moon shining on the snow made everything light up. It was as if we were walking around during an overcast day. The whole area had this gorgeous dark blue-black hue, as snow does during nearly a full moon. As we explored, we found some large Oaks, a meadow and creek and finally, this lone dead looking, twisted tree in the middle of a small clearing. The way the branches arched around each other made it look like a gateway. We all were drawn to it, figuring it was probably an apple tree. When we came to it, I had this impulse to step through the arched branches. As I looked through them, I saw this golden glow in the distance behind the tree line. I stepped through the branches and the glow got brighter and I wanted nothing more than to go to it. My kindred that had been with me, didn't step through the tree and started looking around, wanting to head back to the cabin. One pointed far to the left of the glow that I saw and said she saw the light of the campfire. I asked, "Are you sure? There's a brighter light that way." Pointing to the golden glow. She said she didn't see anything and was sure the way back was the one to the left of the glow that I saw. My other kindred that was with us said he only saw the light to the left. I felt sad as we headed toward the cabin. As if I was missing out on something incredible that would have changed my life. We arrived at the cabin and all night, all I could think about was that glow and wanting so badly to have followed it. I decided that next time we came to Deeply Rooted, I would see the apple tree again.

The next morning, I was packing the last of our things up to head home and as I closed the trunk of my car next to the cabin, I heard a jingling in the woods behind me. When I turned to look, I thought I'd see the grounds keeper's dog, but her car was gone which meant so was her dog and the jingling had sounded like it was in the trees. I had a feeling I was being watched, but didn't see anything as I stared at the branches. The trees were so quiet, it was off putting and I thought something ominous was in the woods. But nothing else happened, so I went back in the cabin and gathered up my daughter and partner to leave. Even as I drove, I had this feeling of dread staring at me from the woods, following me until we left the area.

I'd visited the tree three other times since then. Never at night though, so I never saw that glow again. I'd leave offerings each time, usually something beaded I had crafted to hang in the tree. Occasionally my kindred came with me to offer things too. We found out that fall, that one apple had grown on the tree! Though I guess it produces 1-3 apples every year, we were still excited about it, viewing it as a blessing from the tree.

I recently visited Deeply Rooted for Lughnasadh, completing a Teltown marriage with my partner. It'd been almost a year since I saw the tree since moving to Virginia and I was excited to see it again and give it an offering, still always thinking of that glow and wanting to follow it.

This time, when I stepped through the tree, I had an intense feeling of contentment wash over me. That I was home, an internal voice saying, "Not yet." I knew at that moment that I'd one day go to the Light, that I'd go "home" one day... but not for a very long time. And that was ok.

A storm came through a couple months ago and one of the main branches broke off. It didn't produce anything this year, so we think the tree may be completely dead. We'll see what happens in the future. I still plan to continue giving offerings to the tree.

In hindsight, I know it was a very very dangerous thing I was tempting and still am... I don't know if I really will follow that light one day or if it'll be a good or bad thing, but I know it won't be for a very very long time before that happens." -Amanda

Miscellaneous Experiences

"Growing up in Ireland, I thought that the stories of The Good People and their world were just fairytales to frighten children or something people used to believe hundreds of years ago. As I got older, I started to realise that people like my grandparents and others really believed. The stories they told were not just stories, but real experiences. Then, I started to pay attention to everything my grandparents and older people were saying about their encounters.

Ireland is (or was) for a long time a Catholic or Christian country. We hear a lot about the saints and their stories. For the most part they were real people. However, some of them are incarnations of things much older. Brighíd is an example. And, everyone I knew, whether "Christian" or otherwise, kept many of the ancient pre-Christian ways – even today in modern times. Scratch the surface, and you will find them. The traditions, holy wells, The Days of the Week, the Months of the Year and more in Irish (Gaeilge) are pagan and point to gods, goddesses, fire festivals, and the Good People.

The more I travelled, the more I realised that we could find elementals and sí outside of Ireland, in other countries, and all around the world. Many times, they are unique to the local culture with different names, but they are mostly the same sort.

No matter where I go or what I'm doing, I have the Treoraí Síoga to guide me. Most of the time, I'm unaware of their presence. And, they may not even actually be with me all the time. But, they are always there when I need them.

Saved From Traffic Death

One time a few years ago, I was travelling on holiday in America on one of their big Interstate Highways. We were actually on a parallel road. Driving down the road minding my own business and listening to music, I suddenly had a strong urge to pull over and get off the road. It was definitely unusual, but I did it as quickly as I could. As soon as we were on the side of the road, a huge lorry (18-Wheeler Truck) came speeding by right where we would have been in the road. It was probably going well over 160km/hr (100mph).

A Close Encounter with Na Cúnna Sí

Late one night after the full moon was high, were in an ancient circle in the middle of the woods, which had been in Séamus' family for at least three generations. The woods were connected to a waterway, which connected to a loch. Because of this, we had a slew ofwildlife regularly calling at the circle and our house. However, on this particular night it was different. We completed our rituals and were sharing intimate feelings and stories while enjoying the milseoga agus fíon [desserts and wine]. Suddenly, behind us outside the circle we heard snarling and growling like from a huge animal or dog. But it wasn't natural because of the feeling on the back of my neck and all the hairs on my body shot up. The snarling was moving quickly around in the dark as if there were more than one. It sounded as if you were face to face with a couple of very large wolves or Newfoundlands that were angrily growling and snarling at you. We could feel the deep sounds going through our bodies. We jumped up and I shined the torches into the trees while the commotion and sounds were still going on. Yet, we could see no animals, no movement, no eye shine, or anything. Then, it left as suddenly as it came. We went back to the house and realised we had been gone for over four hours, not just the usual

45 minutes. Early the next morning we went back to the circle and walked all around where we heard the sounds. We did not find any animal hair, animal tracks, or any broken branches or anything. His reconfirmed to us that it must have been at least a couple of Cúnna Sí [fairy hounds] passing through." -Saoirse

The Girl in the Juniper Tree

"In 1966 shortly after my fifth birthday I went out to my maple tree that my dad had moved from the back yard out to the alley behind our back fence. I went and patted my maple tree and turned towards the juniper tree only to see a little Irish girl with sap all over her face crying her heart out... she looked about three years old to me. She was pointing with tears going down her face, so I looked where she was pointing – only to find a neighbor boy whacking on the juniper tree like he was going to take it down. I told him "Don't beat on the tree because it hurt the girl who lived in the tree". He told me that "nobody lived in the tree". I told him "Yes she does, she's a little red headed Irish girl and she is crying". At this point his mother came out and having heard what I said, she told me not to lie, I told her I was not lying and that her son should not be killing trees that had little girls living in them. Then my mom comes out the fence gate and says to the boy's mom "Your son should not be whacking on trees that girls are hiding in, since girls could be hurt if he hits them or if the tree falls down on them". As mom turns me to go back into our yard I tell the little red headed Irish girl to hide in my maple tree because my dad won't let anyone take down my maple tree. I see her walk over to the maple tree and wrap her arms around its slender trunk and vanish into it. Mom gives me the lecture about not telling others about the people in the trees, I ask "Not even the adults?" Mom says "Not even the adults" as "they are not mature enough to understand about the people in the trees." I go "Ohhh" thinking I had better be very careful what I tell the neighbors about if I at five am more mature than the parents where I live. And that was my first introduction to dryads and other members of the People of Peace in Oregon." -Cat

"We have a labyrinth/stone circle where we celebrate the eight neo-pagan holidays. It is our tradition to put out cream for the Fae at these times. One holiday, as we were winding our way out of the labyrinth, carrying our tools (chalice, censer, plate, etc), the chalice lept from the hands of the woman carrying it. I saw it happen. She did not trip, stumble, was not careless. It simply flew from her hands and broke on one of the rocks. We were perplexed. Until we got back into the house and realized that the bowl with the fairy cream was still sitting on the kitchen counter. We concluded that the Good Neighbors definitely wanted their cream!" -Natalie

Assorted Chesapeake Bay Experiences

A Mermaid – In Kilmarnock, on the Chesapeake Bay, there is a cove we used to walk with our dogs. One time it was just a nice late summer day and I began to hear (clairaudience) a sea shanty, so I stopped to listen because there was some familiarity to it (Johnny Sailor Bold). I turned and saw through my vision a mermaid. She had brownish-red hair and was kind of chubby but otherwise somewhat stereotypical. I just pressed my hand to my heart and bowed in acknowledgment but moved on. I have returned to that site since then several times to offer some trinkets I've thought she might like.

A Serpent – The other occurrence on the Chesapeake Bay was crossing the bridge near Newport News to the eastern shore. I just came out of the tunnel so was kind of tranced out a bit and looked over into the water and saw a scaled serpent coiling in on itself. It was big... roiling the water around it and maybe 30' across in that ball. Vivid dark green scales with a lighter green ridge. No mistaking it for anything like a dolphin. As my realization and withdrawal from my fog started to kick in, it was like it realized it was seen and I was nailed with the most intense fear to the point of near paralysis as the panic hit I came to a near stop and kept feeling the pull to drive my truck into the guard rail... it took every miracle to get me off that bridge. I have seen a lot of shit, but the fear that it hurled at me was unlike anything I have ever ever experienced. I'm assuming this was Chessie, but I'm very wary of the Chesapeake Bay/Atlantic now.

Water Spirits – While we lived down that way my daughter also had a ton of encounters and interactions with the waterfolk more upriver who explained they intermarried with the local populations and had clans. We also had a lot of issues with pixies in the house we were renting, dreams of our dogs being stolen, waking to hear tiny bells and insanely tangled hair every morning. Just trouble. The wind also carried a lot of beings, but that might not be what you are asking about.

Miscellaneous Experiences

As we were moving to the hidden valley in the Shenandoah, our first drive there as we entered the gorge I had a massive vision of the rock entity of that area, he appeared like one of those Marvel comic beings made entirely of boulders and rock. He said, "I am older than what they named me" (the range is Massanutten, and there isn't a lot of history to the translation, but he said it in two parts Massa Nauten), so I sensed he was older than the indigenous people (Monacan and later Shawnee diaspora). The valley (Fort Valley) was literally this hidden gem, sparsely populated and still lots of wild. Caves too! We picked up on what felt like clans throughout the valley. Some friendly, some not. Two events happened there that stand out. One night we were getting home late. Our house was mid-way up the ridge and no near neighbors. Across from our home was a field that met the edge of the woods that led up to the ridge. So think, lot of bears, deer…wild. As we came up our road, our driveway was ahead and we could see the length of it as it ran to our house. A huge ball of light was slowly blinking on and off as it moved down our driveway, in front of the fence to the pasture, illuminating it about I would say 4-5′ across… maybe a bit bigger… bright white light. It moved down our driveway and disappeared as we pulled in. There was literally nowhere for it to go as the horse pasture was beyond that and wide open. Still can't debunk it.

We also had waterpeople visit, and I believe they led to the death of one of our dogs. We had two who would come in to the house, mostly to check us out until we warded more specifically since we did not know them. But we used to get drinking water from a natural spring up the road, a locally used place, and got in the habit of leaving coin for when we came. We usually had our dogs and one time I got the distinct impression there was a lot of interest in one of our hounds. He already had a history of seizures, but two days later in a post-ictal state got away from us and drowned in the creek next to our house. I believe with absolute certainty they took him.

We have seen other weird and unidentified lights moving in the area and other very distinct visual and auditory experiences, but like I said, it just goes on and on. This area is wild. I'll add another experience from outside the area that is also interesting.

I was going through a phase about ten years ago when I was deeply into my meditation practices. I was traveling and moving around a lot but wherever I landed I had very vivid dreams of local indigenous spirits, interacting with them, and receiving or exchanging a gift. One of the most clear was in Prescott AZ, south of Flagstaff and the White Mountains, and it was my first night. I dreamed of a group of beings winding their way down a hill, and when they arrived I had a huge bowl of goat milk from which they drank. There was a lot of respectful cheerfulness between us. One of them had the entire lower half of his face, starting at the eyes painted black and he hung back a bit. Kind, smiling but not participating. I suddenly woke to a snowstorm outside." -Hilary

Fairy Man

"In the summer of 2021, I was taking a morning walk, and passing up an alley in my neighborhood. As I approached the end of the block, I saw a young man pass by. He seemed ordinary; not handsome or ugly, brown hair, wearing jeans and a Celtic-design t-shirt, carrying a small back-pack. He glanced at me, stopped, and said, "water dragon?" I said, "Why, yes" because that is the year in which I was born. We chatted for a few minutes, then he walked off briskly, and was soon out of sight. I continued with my walk, and a block or so later, he suddenly reappeared, from a completely different direction than I'd last seen him. When he came up to me, I asked, "Why did you call me that?" He mumbled something about "I had reminded him of a friend", then knelt down and opened his pack, offering "take whatever you like". There were fascinating things in the pack, but what I remember best was a glowing amber sphere, about the size of a golf ball. I was not about to touch it. I said, "Oh, you are very generous, but I already have many interesting things." An annoyed expression crossed his face, and for the first time he looked directly at me, and I saw his eyes, like those of a hawk, and almost as golden as the amber sphere. (His "mask" may have slipped for a moment?) He picked up the pack, and without another word strode briskly away. I have never seen him again. (I quite deliberately did not say "thank you", but used the phrase "you are generous.")" -Rowan

Fairy Hound

"Other encounter – a few years back, I was stretched out on my couch reading in mid-afternoon, and heard a soft clicking, as of small dog claws on the wooden floor. I glanced up, and saw a small white dog, a little larger than a guinea pig, trot briskly out of the hallway, across the living room, into the dining room, and thence out of sight into the kitchen, where the sound ceased. The two cats with me – one curled up on my stomach, and the other on the back of the couch – turned their heads and tracked the creature, but did not seem upset by it. After the clicking ceased, I got up and looked; nothing. Had it not been for the reaction of the cats, I might have thought I had imagined it. This was not a ghost-dog, but something quite different. It appeared solidly physical, and did not seem to notice me as it passed through. I have never seen it again, though I have once or twice heard the clicking claws, usually late at night." -Rowan

Three Stories

"I live in the province of New Brunswick, Canada. New Brunswick, as with Newfoundland, Nova Scotia and Prince Edward Island has a very long history of Irish, Scottish, Welsh and English emigrants.

For the sake of context and ambience, I'd like to give a description of where these events occurred. I owned a mini-home (aka trailer with a pitched roof) on my piece of land during 2006 – 2021. I still refer to it as my home even though it was sold in 2021. This is a rural area and my home sits about 18 yards from the elbow bend of a river. A small graveyard is about 33 yards from my home. Open field, abandoned farm house/barns and old trees surround the property. The trailer was built in 1972. This whole section of that immediate area is Theirs (I should add that the Dead play a role in this as well). My daily life was filled with countless interactions and escapades with the Good Folk. I've never been happier in my life. I was welcomed by Them and They opened for me the deepest experiences and training that I could have ever imagined. I always understood that my role was to pay the land taxes and keep the home clean and viable. Due to my health and age (67) I had to sell this precious liminal home in 2021. It's been two and a half years since I left and the 'new owners' have not moved in. This home sits empty of human life and has fallen into disarray.

Tale #1) To get to my home I have to drive past the graveyard and along an old two lane twisty road. This road separates the graveyard and river on one side, and my home/Their land on the other. I was driving home one day, along this road just across from the graveyard and I suddenly felt myself start to shift from everyday awareness-vision to Seer awareness. I heard many of Them yelling 'SLOW DOWN!' About 10 yards in front of me I suddenly see one of Them and I'm about to drive right into Them. I'll never forget the look of shock on Their face and I know that my mouth was hanging open in disbelief. I assume that They were coming back from the graveyard, attempting to cross the road. They were surrounded by a blueish shimmering energy. They were of thin build, about 5'8" (?), human looking, very pale complexion, dark hair, black tight long-sleeved turtleneck top and black tight pants. In the instant that all of this happened, I felt as though we were both suspended in time and place. Our physical motion seemed frozen. I don't recall being able to brake my car or physically move. They were stationary, frozen with legs and arms opened wide, suspended above the road by a couple of feet, as if They had been running across the road. In a flash of an instant, I regained movement and They continued running across the road and into the field, with the shimmering blue energy following in Their wake. I've no idea why this happened as it did or how it happened. Soon after this jarring event, They did make me clean up all of the litter and garbage humans had thrown along the road side that connected to Their land. My human neighbours thought that I was doing this for them! I just smiled and nodded politely. LOL

Tale #2) One very sunny, calm autumn day I was raking up my backyard near the house. I was so very pleased with myself for being so efficient. If there was a breeze in the air at all, it was not obvious. I was very serious and focused on my extremely important task. At one point I stopped raking and started walking toward a different patch of grass, and I was suddenly pushed backward quite hard, almost falling to the ground. A very strong, very concentrated blast of wind took the rake right out of my hand and pushed the self-satisfaction out of me too! There really was no natural wind .... I started laughing while realizing what had happened. My mundane day to day life seemed to be a never-ending supply of humour to Them. LOL

Tale #3) My home is triangular shape, 66'x14'. The longer length of it sits firmly and clearly in a North – South direction. One evening I was laying in bed watching TV. I started hearing music coming from outside, east direction, middle of the house area. At first, I couldn't clearly hear it. I muted the TV and I got out of bed. I was intending to open the curtains on that east side of the house, expecting to see people walking along the road in the dark. Once I clearly was able to hear the music, I stopped short and hopped back into bed. I heard a very simple, brief melodic tune. Seemingly one or two instruments (as if I'd know!). The tune was repeated a few times, two, three? Previously, on several different occasions I have heard the music of the Good Folk. This is what was now happening. I was captured in this bliss and saw/felt Them move from the east side of the house to the south side. And once again this melodic tune was played and repeated. And once again They moved around the house to the west side and stood right outside of my bedroom window. Again, the tune was played and repeated. I stood before my closed curtains trying to raise my hand to open them. I felt such excitement! I had no fear of being harmed. It was more the case that I felt that my sanity was at risk if I opened the curtains. Once again, They moved along the west side of the house, arriving at the north side. The tune played, repeated and to my knowledge They left. I cannot describe this experience without attempting to describe the physical experience of hearing Their music. When I hear Their music the immediate air pressure around me seems to change, intensify. I feel somehow locked, transfixed, detached yet physically present within my immediate surroundings. The musical vibrations seem to travel from the instrument to my ear moving at a different time-frame than my immediate surroundings, yet feeling like quite an everyday experience. I have been able to 'see' the music vibration as it moves towards me. Once it hits my body it feels physical, as if it were a rope lassoing me and holding me. When I've heard Their music, I feel I am on a knife edge of utter ecstasy and the terror of being keenly aware of my mortality. If I've learned anything, it is surely to know how blessed I am and how precious my human life is." -Teididh

Profit and Loss – An Encounter with the Aos Sidhe

"Several years ago, my personal spiritual practice abruptly changed to a focus on the Aos Sidhe and one of Their queens, Áine. Some dramatic circumstances and revelations led to this, but that's a different story or two. Along with this change came a new focus for my creative life. I am a singer-songwriter in a duo with my husband, and we record professionally as Neptune's Keep. Queen Áine is well known in folklore as a muse to poets and musicians, and early in my association with her I was given an assignment: create and record three albums of music that would tell the stories of the Sidhe. After careful consideration I consented, and Neptune's Keep began working in earnest on the first album. Over the next two years, song after song came to me, downloaded pretty much intact into my brain from what I felt must be an Otherworldly source. As I received the songs,

I transcribed, arranged, sang and recorded them with Stu in collaboration with a professional recording studio. This was ultimately a very involved, two-year project.

In October of the first year of the project, I had my first physical encounter with the Aos Sidhe. It was Halloween night, which, as a Druid, I celebrated as Samhain. This was my first Samhain since "signing on" with Áine, so that evening I performed a ceremony dedicated to The Good People and my Sidhe muse. I did this alone in a room on the second floor of our house. That room gets warm, so I left a window open during the event. Just as I finished the ceremony, I became aware of music wafting in the open window from outdoors. It seemed to emanate from no particular direction; it just floated in on the breeze. At first the music was so soft that I couldn't make out just what it was. Then it got slightly louder, and I could hear the tune. To my surprise, note for note what wafted into my room was a traditional Irish jig!

I looked out the window, up and down the street, but I saw no one – no trick-or-treaters, no evidence of a party in the neighborhood. And in our neighborhood, nobody was likely to have any idea what a traditional Irish jig is, much less be listening to one on Halloween night! It felt very strange. But, seeking a rational explanation, I considered that Stu might be practicing his dulcimer downstairs with his own window open. Stu had played professionally with another duo for many years, and Celtic dance music was one of their mainstays. I walked downstairs and found Stu sitting at his computer in his office. I asked him "What was that jig you were just playing on the dulcimer? I didn't recognize it."

He said "I wasn't playing the dulcimer."

"Were you playing a video on the computer?"

"Nope. I've just been sitting here typing."

"Well, have you ever heard this jig?" And I sang the tune to him.

"I have never heard that one, but it's certainly a proper jig!" And then I knew: the only possible source for that strange, elusive music was The Good People Themselves. They gave it to me, not just as a musical thought, but as a physical presence, right into my human ears! And that experience corroborated what I had believed all along; that the Otherworldly music taking over my life was not just a figment of my own fertile imagination. It was of the Aos Sidhe. That tune is now known as Merrymakers' Samhain, soon to be included on an upcoming Neptune's Keep album.

Fast forward another year, and we come to the second, darker part of this story. For many years I had been working with a singing coach to improve my skills. At first Lionel and I met at his studio, but with the advent of COVID, all our lessons moved online to Zoom. By then we knew each other well and had become very close friends. We both looked forward to our twice monthly schmoozing and singing sessions. Lionel worked tirelessly with me on each of the 13 songs on our album of musical Sidhe folklore. And I taught him a lot about The Good People and their stories. During a Zoom get-together when the album was about 2/3 complete, I shared a music video with Lionel. A good friend of mine, a Sami singer-songwriter, had made a marvelous little musical film which told a story of the Ulda. (You can view the video on YouTube: https://youtu.be/dxkeAJecrWQ) The Ulda are among the Sami "fairies," and many of their stories are very similar to those of The Sidhe. A common theme is the abduction of human children, and that was the plot of this music video: on a picnic at the edge of a lake by a woods, some human children are lured away by The Ulda. An adult at the picnic is also enticed when an Ulda whispers in his ear.

Lionel watched the film with fascination. In the very last scene, the parents realize their children have disappeared. The adults get up to search, and the man who heard the Ulda stands staring into the woods. There the film ends. When we finished watching, Lionel said "At the end of the film, when the man goes into the woods and suddenly disappears, is it implied that he left with the fairies?"

A little perplexed, I said "The man doesn't disappear. The film ends with him just staring into the woods."

"But I saw him disappear before my eyes!" Lionel protested. "I know what I saw!" So we watched the film again. The second time, Lionel saw exactly what I saw – the man did not disappear. Lionel insisted "I know what I saw the first time, and it was completely different the second time."

With some gravitas, I said "They – Themselves – changed it for your eyes."

Then Lionel, my very practical Voice Specialist with a PhD in Vocal Science replied, "I think you have convinced me that these fairy people are real!"

I wish I had realized the full import of that experience. I wish I had understood the message in that video, sent to Lionel by Otherworldly forces. Since the very inception of our Sidhe music project, I personally had encountered perilous opposition from forces opposed to it – presumably Queen Áine's enemies. But somehow, I failed to see the simple threat to Lionel implicit in that film: "This album the two of you are working on? We do not want it made. If you continue to work with this woman on this music, we can make you disappear, too." And then they did.

A few weeks after this incident, Lionel had a strange, apparently neurological "event" in which he behaved irrationally near his home and was unresponsive when a neighbor tried to find out what was wrong. It sounded like a stroke, but subsequent medical examination found no evidence of one, and nothing medically amiss.

A few weeks after that incident, Lionel quite suddenly disappeared from the face of the Earth. On a day when we were scheduled for a Zoom session, he called me on the phone. He was clearly upset and said that he was at his financial institution and would have to reschedule with me because he had been the victim of identity theft. That was the last time he ever spoke to me. For months I and many others among his close friends and students tried unsuccessfully to contact him, and no one knew what had happened to him. Lionel was a very loving and giving person, and I KNOW he would not willingly have abandoned us all.

Finally, about a year ago a picture of Lionel appeared on his Facebook page – a photo taken at a recent political event. It was clear that, though still alive, the dear Lionel we all knew was gone. He was literally a shade of who he had been. Since then, there's been absolutely no news of him at all. We assume he had a massive stroke that basically wiped away his personality and memory. I believe he was elf-shot in retribution for the work he and I were doing for Queen Áine of The Sidhe.

The first album in Neptune's Keep's series of Sidhe music was released on Winter Solstice 2022. My work for Themselves has continued and will continue. I just wish the price exacted for that work had not been so steep. And I will carry that loss always." -Crow Bard

Angels

"It was sometime around 2001. It was the weekend and I was having a sleepover at my friend J's house. To give you some background on the neighborhood, her house was a few minutes from mine in the newer section of my grandparents' neighborhood. So, within walking distance but it was easier to bike or drive. My grandparents built their house around the 40s or 50s. When my mom was growing up, J's side of the neighborhood was still blackberry and raspberry bushes where my mom and aunt would go berry picking. My parents built their house in the 70s, and shortly after is when J's area began development. The reason why I include these details is because I think it's interesting to note that so much paranormal activity happened between our three houses despite the area being so historically insignificant.

Things were weird pretty much from the beginning. I arrived at her house in the late afternoon/early evening. Her parents were going to be out late, so we had the house to ourselves. It was just us and her mom's tiny dog. We were mostly hanging out in her room on the second floor at first. It was a pretty normal teenage room aside from the antique furniture and the creepy doll collection. J only had a twin-size bed so we had laid blankets and pillows on the floor in front of the bed to sleep on. We were probably just listening to music or reading about her love life with tarot cards or something when J got this really weird look in her eye and said, "Lindsey... an angel is going to visit you tonight."

I remember just sitting there on the floor, looking between her face and a crayon drawing on the closet door, while a feeling like a bucket of ice water went down my spine. I was raised pretty agnostically/atheistically... but I'd had enough weird experiences all my life (and I'd been into witchcraft since the mid-90s) to believe that there was more to this world. I just didn't view it through a religious lens. I remember thinking at the time that 1. I didn't trust that it was actually an angel that was going to visit (J was into a unique combination of Christianity and paganism at this time, so I feel like she interpreted it as an angel because of this), 2. Something real was definitely going to visit, 3. I don't think it was completely J who said that to me (like something had influenced her/taken her over for a split second), and 4. I was a total wuss at the prospect of seeing whatever it was.

The conversation moved along eventually and something made us want to get on the internet. This was back in the dial-up AOL days so only the computer in her mom's bedroom was hooked up to the internet. It was directly across the hall from J's room. I remember walking in there and casually glancing to my left and seeing like a giant floor to ceiling dark green curtain. I went to ask J what was behind it, but when I looked back it was just a small window, like all the others on the second floor. It was weird, but I just chalked it up to my eyes playing tricks on me.

On our way back to J's room, I remember noticing a door to my left, before the staircase. Now I was fairly familiar with J's mom's house. The stairs were in the center of the hall upstairs. If you were walking up the stairs, in front of you to the left was the linen closet. In front to the right was the bathroom. J's room was at the end of the hall to the left, her parents' room was at the end of the hall on the right. Directly to the left of the stairs, on the wall opposite of the linen closet, was a door to the spare room. This new, mystery room would be directly to the right of the stairs on the wall opposite of the bathroom. As we were walking, I asked her what was in that room. She said, "what room?" And, of course, when I turned around there was no door there. In fact, the wall there wasn't even a foot long. It would be impossible for a door to have been there.

Fast forward to us getting ready to sleep. So, we're both lying down on our blankets. She's on the side near the interior wall and I'm on the side near the window. J fell asleep pretty fast but I was still awake, consumed with anxiety about my supposed angelic visitor. I remember looking out the window, staring at the trees and the moonlight. For whatever reason, I let my vision trail past the window to the left (towards the corner of the room). There was a red glowing ball, about the size of a mush ball, just chilling there in the air in the corner of her room less than a foot from the ceiling. My initial thought was that it was the moonlight reflecting off of the bottle of Code Red Mountain Dew that was by my head. But I kept thinking that that didn't make sense. It should be a shaft of light, not a ball. I looked back over to the window to see if there was anything red over there, and that's when I caught the bright green light out of my peripheral vision.

Right next to me was a person-sized mass of bright green light (just a shade darker than neon green). It wasn't a perfect sphere and it wasn't in the air. It looked vaguely like the shape of a small person squatting next to me (maybe around four feet tall if they had been standing), except there wasn't any light where the head would be. I remember being terrified... but J was asleep and no one else was home. It felt like a warm hand touched my left cheek, while I had a cold, wet sensation on my lower right rib cage. I don't know if I thought this at the time, but I always associate it with the idea of a cold, metal scalpel nowadays. I decided to nope out of this by turning towards J and pulling the blanket over my head. I curled up under the blanket and silently freaked out for a bit while wishing J would just wake up (don't ask me why I was so reluctant to just wake her up myself. I couldn't tell you. I think I was almost afraid to say anything out loud lest I provoked this light lump into action. I felt frozen to inaction by my fear.

So, at some point I must have fallen asleep because I remember waking up, still under the blanket and facing J, to sort of catch the tail end of myself saying something as if I'd been talking in my sleep. But I have no idea what was said. Then I heard J respond... it was all nonsense words. Lots of "amma, alla, anna" sounds. I lifted a corner of the blanket off my face so I could see her and strained to hear what she was saying. All of a sudden my hearing filled with white noise, like radio static, completely blocking out any other sound and maybe creating a mild pressure. And then I hear directly in my head over the static this deep male voice say, "You bitch you bitch you bitch"... then everything stops. My hearing is normal again, J isn't talking in her sleep any longer, and it feels like a weight has been lifted from the room. I stare at J, practically willing her to wake up so I can talk about this. She does so after a few minutes and I explained what happened. She didn't experience anything, but she believed me and were freaked out too. I told her I needed to use the bathroom but I didn't want to go alone. She had to go too, so it worked out.

We walked down the hall to the bathroom and noticed the door was completely shut and the lights were off (which wasn't normal when it wasn't in use). We heard her dog from inside the bathroom and started freaking out a little again. It didn't make sense. This dog was her mom's spoiled baby. Her parents were home at this point and asleep in their room with the door shut. The bathroom is right next to their room as I mentioned earlier. If the dog had been bothering them, it wouldn't make sense to lock it in the room next door (without food or water). It would have made more sense to lock it in the bathroom downstairs or the basement. But furthermore, we couldn't imagine her mom ever locking the dog up regardless of how much it was yapping. When we opened the door and turned on the light, we found that the dog's leash (he often wore it inside) was shoved under the toilet. Almost dead center. There were bits of grouting all over the floor and the dog was freaking out. It took the combined strength of both me and J pulling to free the leash.

The only way I could imagine the dog's leash getting stuck under there would be if the dog was running around the toilet in circles and at some point the leash snagged on something... but even though the dog was tiny, it was not tiny enough to get behind the toilet, making that theory a bust. Plus, the grouting had literally been removed and was scattered around the floor in order for the leash to be shoved under there. I personally believe that whatever it was that was messing with us that night had purposely done this to the dog to keep it from waking us up and interrupting its plans. We tried asking her mom about it the next morning and she just blew us off like, "Oh, I'm sure the dog just bumped the door" or something. I just remember not

---

getting any satisfactory answers because if she had simply said she had put the dog in the bathroom, it wouldn't be as weird.

I've always associated the red and green lights as two separate beings, I just wasn't able to fully perceive them. The more I've read about lore and other people's encounters, the more I find it interesting that the red one was essentially a "tall being" but I was only seeing where the head would be, and the green one was essentially a "short being", yet I could see everything BUT the head. Also, the part where I was touched – somehow I completely forgot about this part, despite or because of how terrifying it was, until I read my old diary entry about the incident." -Lindsey

The Wild Hunt

"This happened while I was on maternity leave. I couldn't tell you if it was Nov, Dec 2020, or Jan, Feb 2021. All I remember is that it was winter, but it had been dry and maybe a bit warm. I fell asleep on the daybed in my daughter's room with her in my arms. A really weird storm was happening outside. It was snow/rain and lightning. Loud crashes of thunder. And very, very strong wind. It creeped me out and I was half worried we'd get a tornado warning. Kiddo had an Owlet monitor. If you didn't have one for your kids, it's a band that straps on their foot and monitors oxygen and pulse to prevent SIDS.

I can't remember the exact order of events... I may have woken up before the monitor went off or it could have been what woke me up. But I remember it beeping and struggling to wake my daughter. I remember thunder and lightning and so much wind. I did get her awake eventually. And I swear to god I heard a horse neigh outside and hooves on the roof along with the gusting wind. My mind kept singing *Riders on the Storm* by The Doors and I just kept thinking, "The Wild Hunt".

Now, the Owlet has had a number of false alarms when it's been loose and she could have just been in a deep sleep. But

I don't know... I definitely did not imagine the sound of the horse." -Lindsey

A Banshee Story

"My maternal grandmother's side of the family came to America at the time of the Great Famine, and settled in upstate Pennsylvania, in the coal-mining region. In 1918, my grandmother lost two of her brothers to the influenza pandemic.

The story goes that my great-uncle Michael Buggy was dying. He was only 21; his younger brother had already died. The family was gathered one night as he lay dying upstairs. There was a knock at the door, and a man entered. He said he was a doctor, and was let upstairs into Michael's room. The doctor was up there for a while, then came downstairs, and said, "There's someone here keeping this boy from dying. You have to let him go." The doctor then left. Outside, this unearthly wail went up – which my aunt explained was the keening of the bean sídhe. That night, my great-uncle died." -Mary

A Long Hallway to the Bean Sí

"I've been thinking about this a lot lately, so I'm grateful for the opportunity to share this experience. I've been doing a lot of trauma and self-healing work this last year, and a big part of it has involved bringing up otherwise repressed memories of aspects of my sometimes less than ideal childhood. The following account has never been far from my mind. Nor has my memory or retelling of the account wavered. It is, as far as I can tell, my second or third earliest memory in life. Here it is.

I remember spending a lot of time as a child at my grandparent's house near Winter Park in Central Florida. I remember a lot of things from that time: large family gatherings, swimming in their pool, watching my favorite cartoons on their tv, my grandfather's chronic illness and its effect on himself and the family, walks to the lake to feed the ducks with my grandmother, and the near nightly recurring dream of long conversations with a much older, white-haired woman.

This is the dream. It would always start in the same place. I be in the far bedroom in their house where I would sleep when visiting, and likely was sleeping at the time I dreamed this. I would take a walk down the hallway towards the family room and kitchen. The hallway though was immensely larger in the dream than in real life. The proportions of the whole house were 'off'.

Passing into the common area and in the kitchen passthrough area I would see Her; ghostly ethereal, incorporeal, wispy and levitating. Never was She what I would describe as a welcome visage in my incredibly young mind. The 'morality' of my family seemed to instill upon me a fear of anything that was 'other' or 'different'. This woman was definitely of the appearance I had been taught would be called 'evil'. Or, in the parlance of the Satanic Panic of the time: Demonic. Funnily enough, this early time in my life was when I first began to question my gender. But I digress.

So, I'm in the dreaming, in an impossibly sized version of my grandmother's kitchen, talking to a 'ghost' (how I knew Her at this time). I was never permitted, or allowed myself, to remember the details of our conversation precisely. The conversation always moved to my grandparent's bedroom in this dream. Usually, me sitting in the chair that existed in the corner of the room while we talked. All I really remembered was Her telling me that she had my Soul, wanted my Soul, or would come after my Soul. Something along those lines.

It was incredibly jarring. Nothing in my life up to this point prepared me for this experience. This dream reoccurred for three months. Every night. I know this because another of my oldest and firmest memories is of me finally breaking down and asking my grandmother how to stop it. In retrospect, she was probably one of the few people in my family I could have asked and been met with an open and honest understanding that was so pure as to put me at ease.

Her advice, as my family was pretty intensely Catholic, was to pray to the Holy Spirit for the dreams to go away. I did, and the dreams did. All was well. Except it wasn't. I won't go in to details on everything that's happened between then and now but all I can say is: Don't bury your dreams. You do yourself a great disservice when you do that. I never forgot this part of my life, no matter how hard I tried.

So, how did I know it was a Bean Sí? Well, I really only discovered Paganism was a 'thing' in 2020. Complete with amazing people, rich literature, and a thriving culture. It was after meeting some those folks, and making some amazing friends, that I was inspired to go look for my own answers.

It took me three and a half years to get up the courage to face my past. I remembered from the dream that the ghostly woman I was talking to in those dreams all those years ago had used the form of a minor villain character from a cartoon I was very fond of at that time in my life. Just this last year (summer 2023) after going all-in on Paganism in 2021 I finally worked up the courage to both locate a copy of that particular 80's cartoons archives and watched 20 or so episodes until I stumbled across the episode with that character the dream character used. It was a Bean Sí, or Banshee.

I'm certain I now know who She was. That She did indeed want me to come looking for my Soul. I believe we've since had a lot of conversations about what I needed to do to get it back. I believe She was there when I found it again. I also believe that there are many valid paths to one's soul that anyone may undertake. She helped me find a Jungian/Wiccan/Qabalistic amalgam that seemed to work in my case.

So, what's my take away on this? A few things stand out: It's ok to be afraid. It's ok to grieve. It's ok to be you. Don't run from your dreams. Even if they seem scary, or better than you ever believed they could be. Allow vulnerability. Don't judge anything by its outward appearance, or by how society and media say you should. And, most importantly: When it is time to cross the ford, you're going to be fine. Thank you for allowing me the space to share this story, and aspects of my life." -Michelle

These stories have been presented here as they were given to me, with minimal editing, to show readers the range of contemporary material. They are only a small slice of the fairy experiences that occur in North America today and offer some particular perspectives, but show the way that the beliefs continue to exist and even thrive.

Chapter 7

Blurry Lines

One thing that adds some difficulty in discussing this subject is wrestling with the definition of what is or is not a fairy and how closely linked to the Celtic cultures' fairies might be. While it has certainly become a trope to assume that fairies must be Irish, Scottish, Welsh, etc., it's worth remembering that the term itself was originally French and that stories of fairies can be found in continental Europe as well as Ireland and the UK. Perhaps ironically the term fairy has, in this context, returned to its older use, being applied to any unknown supernatural being or experience that can't easily be categorized.

In seeking modern encounters, I asked people to reach out if they had any experience with a Celtic fairy in North America, and many people wanted clarification on what I meant by both Celtic and fairy, to which I always responded that I was leaving it up to the responder to define those terms for themselves. I was not trying to dictate who or what might fit into this book, but to look at the body of belief that exists out there already. If a person felt that what they had encountered was Celtic and/or a fairy then that was what mattered.

In some accounts discussed in the 2018 Fairy Census the person reporting the story stated that they didn't know for certain that what they experienced was a fairy but that the word fairy seemed the best one to describe what they'd seen. Others described beings that were vastly at odds with Celtic folklore but nonetheless strongly believed these beings were fairies; as one respondent put it: *"When you know [it is a fairy], you know. You can feel it in your heart."* (Young, 2018, p 197). This intuitive approach to understanding who and what fairies are or may be is a common one across the more modern material that I looked at.

Sometimes we have no name or context for something we experience. I often have people come to me with encounters they've had with various beings, looking for names for what they've encountered or cultural context to understand them through. It's understandable. It's human nature to want names for things and to seek understand what we've experienced by relating it to a body of existing knowledge. When we first see a new animal, we might have the same urge to find a name for it and seek out basic information about it. The problem we can run into though with personal experiences is that even with the amazing store of folklore we have sometimes we encounter things that have no names and no known stories.

When people run into these unnamed or unknown spirits and realize that they are unknown there is often a tendency to react by doubting themselves. As if just because the spirit they encountered can't be easily named and categorized the person themselves can no longer trust what they experienced. I think we need to be careful not to fall into that mindset that the only spirits and Otherworldly beings who exist are the ones who have already been recorded and defined by previous human generations; remember that even in the mortal world humans still sometimes discover new species. In the same way when we encounter the Otherworld and its inhabitants, we should keep in mind that not everything there is known and defined by human understanding – indeed I would argue that its hubris to think that humans have such a complete understanding of the Otherworld as all that. Folklore and folk belief are fluid and changeable and by their nature adapt over time. Just as we can trace the changes across time to today, we must also factor in the impact of people's personal experiences that defy our current body of knowledge.

And that's still alright. A personal experience is no less valid just because what you saw or experienced can't be found in a book or wasn't shared by other people you know. I'd suggest (as always) making notes about the experience, what you saw, how it acted, what happened, and so on because that might be useful later in discerning at least the nature of what you encountered. But don't worry that just because you can't find it in a folklore book or grimoire that it doesn't exist. There's a lot more out there than can be found between the pages of books and all folklore begins somewhere.

I'd like to wrap this chapter up with seven things you should keep in mind about fairies going forward which may help sort out whether an experience is or is not a fairy:

1. The Word Fairy Is a Catchall Term – Although we use fairy as if it were specific the word is and has always been a generic term applied to a range of beings. Its history goes back 700 years in English and it was used interchangeably with elf, goblin, imp, and incubus for most of its history; the oldest meaning of fairy related to the place and later as an adjective for beings from or with the nature of that place. There are seem groups who use fairy now to indicate a specific type of being, what Paracelsus would have called Sylphs, but across the breadth of folklore and academia the word is still used as a catch all. This is important to know because when you see an older account talking about a fairy encounter, or a journal article talking about fairies, or the word fairy used to translate a term like the Korean yojeong it is inevitably being used in the wider generic sense, not for a small sprite.

2. The Unseelie and Seelie Courts Are Uniquely Scottish – Appearing in urban fantasy of the late 20th century as a ubiquitous division of all fairies into a sort of 'good' and 'bad' grouping, the idea of the Seelie and Unseelie courts comes from

Scottish folklore specifically. As much as its popular today – and sometimes convenient – to divide all fairy beings by these arbitrary lines, in folklore we do not find the concepts outside of the areas they originated in, that is, specifically, in the southern areas of Scotland. The words themselves come from Scots and have a long and interesting history as applied to fairies, which goes far beyond a simple good/bad dichotomy. This is important to know for two reasons: firstly, because the terms apply, really, only to Scottish folklore and not elsewhere, and secondly following that because when you see them being applied elsewhere – for example, a book or article talking about Irish fairy beings or monarchs being in one court or another, or claiming English fairy monarchs rule either court – it's a red flag that what you are reading is fiction not folklore.

3. Fairies Have Their Own Rules – One thing that is clearly established across every and all stories we have of the Good Folk is that they do not adhere to human ethics or rules but operate on their own system of both. Many of these seem to contradict human expectations, such as the prohibition we find in some folklore not to say thank you or not to acknowledge seeing the Good Folk. These rules are not homogenous and will vary by specific group of Otherworldly beings and by the wider culture they are associated with, but in general it can be said that fairy etiquette will always be different from and often at odds with human norms. There is often a double standard that seems to exist as well across fairy folklore where the ways that humans are treated and the ways that humans are expected to act are not the same rules applied to fairies themselves. Humans often find these beings cruel or capricious at least in part because of this difference in behaviour and expectation, which we may perhaps describe as 'cultural differences'. This fact is important to know because it helps put the wider folklore in context and provides a basis for interactions.

4. Cultural Lenses Make a Huge Difference – Despite the way that the word is used generically what we would call fairies in various cultures are often very different and those differences matter. Just as knowing that the seelie and unseelie are uniquely Scottish concepts we find that many details of fairylore are particular to specific cultures or locations. If we say that fairy is an umbrella term under which, for example, would fall beings like the Tylwyth Teg (Welsh), Daoine Sith (Scottish), and Daoine Uaisle (Irish) then we must expect there will be differences in how each group is described, understood, and interacted with in the stories we have. The Irish Daoine Uaisle are not English fairies nor are they the Welsh Tylwyth Teg, and we have to be aware of that and cautious about over homogenizing everything. While there are cross cultural similarities, we must be careful not to assume from a few similar details that the entirety is the same. A good example of this would be the Cú Sidhe (Irish fairy hound), Cú Sithe (Scottish Fairy Hound), and Cwn Annwn (Welsh fairy hound), all of which broadly fit a wider category of 'fairy hound' but which each have different descriptions, behaviours, and stories. This is important to know in the same way it's important to know that, when you visit a different country, things won't be the same as they are where you live – cultural nuances matter and help us understand stories in different ways.

5 A Lot of Our Ideas About Fairies Today Come from Media Not Folklore – The popular image of a fairy – winged, pointy eared, tiny – although working its way into folklore comes from somewhere else as we discussed in Chapter 5. In fact, up until the last few decades, anecdotal accounts describe very, very different beings than what we find in popular stories today. These all combined in various ways across art and fiction over the last hundred years and are now found in modern anecdotal accounts, as the media we consume shapes our expectations and perceptions of fairy experiences. This is important to know because when reading older accounts or modern accounts from places with extant fairylore generally the beings described have none of these features and knowing that may help you if you have a personal experience which would fit the criteria of a fairy but which you dismiss because there were no wings or pointed ears.

6 Fairies as Nature Spirits Are a New Idea – While the idea of fairies as nature spirits has become very popular it's actually a fairly new idea, rooted in the late 19th century. Theosophy, beginning in the late 19th century, looked to the views of Paracelsus about elemental spirits and blended them with the Victorian romanticism of nature to give us the fairy as embodiment of and protector of the natural world which has become so popular today. It is true if we look to Greek or Roman cultures that we can find beings like dryads and naiads who are spirits of specific natural features, but I would argue that the classical understanding of these beings is not the same as the modern concept of a nature spirit. In any event the Celtic language speaking cultures specifically do not seem to have any equivalent concept, with their Otherworldly spirits being territorial of specific places or things (wells, tress, rocks) but not as aspects or spirits literally of those things; in fact, we have multiple stories across Ireland, Scotland, and England of the fairies moving their homes or leaving a place in a way that a nature spirit by definition could not do. This is important, not to dissuade people who choose to believe in nature spirits as fairies, but so that everyone can have a wider context for these beings that is open to multiple options and aware of the history of specific beliefs.

7 They Aren't Evil – But They Aren't Good Either – There are two popular views of fairies that float around:

1. They are extremely dangerous and must be avoided at all cost.
2. They are benevolent spirit guides that exist to aid humans.

As is usual with this subject, the truth is both and neither. We have a lot of folklore and anecdotal accounts of fairies causing harm to humans, sometimes as retribution sometimes because they wanted to. And by harm, I mean blinding humans, giving them painful long-term illnesses, driving them mad, or straight up murdering them. On the other hand, we also have lots of folklore and anecdotal accounts of fairies acting benevolently, healing humans, giving them luck or money, providing essential blessings. Are they evil? No. Are they good? Also no. They are diverse and from a human perspective often mercurial and unpredictable. I have talked to people who are adamant that they have interacted with fairies for a long time and only ever had good experiences and I am not denying that that can be true, dependent on what exactly you are interacting with, but there are also people who have the opposite experience and their accounts are just as valid. Or put another way one person's good experiences don't negate someone else's bad experiences and vice versa – there's a lot of nuance here. The takeaway is that these beings aren't simple and they are never clearly one thing or another.

Conclusion

Across the last several centuries we can find stories of Celtic cultural fairies in many places outside Western Europe, carried there by the people who came from Europe and believed in these spirits. They dance across the pages of literature and poetry, they are found in newspaper articles and in place names, they linger at the edges of folk stories and they glide through modern anecdotes in defiance of disbelief. They persist, as the fairies of the Celtic language speaking cultures persist, at the fringes of our understanding and in the shadows of more popular tales. But they do persist.

The fairies of the diaspora, however, aren't the fairies of Western Europe, just as the diaspora itself, in its various manifestations isn't the original culture that it grew from. The fairies of North America instead are in many ways their own concept and the beliefs about them, while similar, are divergent from the older European ones. In Ireland you wouldn't invite fairies into your home – indeed the bulk of belief centres on keeping them out – but in the Irish American diaspora there is a certain assumption that fairies may be present and even an embracing of that presence (Daimler, 2023). In the 1860's New York changeling case[31] the mother, herself an Irish immigrant, believed that fairy presence in the house was a sign of her son having been exchanged for a changeling child. But there is no such belief found in Ireland, contemporary to the case or since, that would support that as a sign of a changeling. Her attempts to drive off the changeling with iron and fire, however, are in line with Irish methods (Woodyard & Young, 2019). These two examples illustrate the related but divergent nature of fairy belief between the two continents.

In writing this book I haven't attempted to offer an exhaustive study of North American fairy beliefs which can be traced back to Europe – it would require a much longer text to do that – but have offered a range of evidence to show that these beliefs have existed and do still exist outside of traditionally Celtic cultural areas. In some places this folklore is quite thin on the ground, it's true, while in others it is much easier to find, but it is there as it had been for around four hundred years. As European cultures colonized North America and as waves of various immigrants arrived from places that held strong fairy beliefs, we find those beliefs appearing in Canada, the US, and to a lesser degree Mexico. Teasing out the exact sources of these beliefs and the influences which have shaped them through the 21st century shows that while there are other factors and cultures at play there is a notable Celtic presence.

Ultimately the simple answer to whether there are Celtic fairies in North America is a clear and unequivocal 'yes', however, it is worth appreciating the nuances that we have discussed in this book, the range of evidence, and the way that North American fairy belief differs from the original beliefs which they branched off from.

Endnotes

1. Merriam Webster Dictionary defines diaspora as a group of people who have settled away from their traditional country or area https://www.merriam-webster.com/dictionary/diaspora

2. There are, for example, a range of beliefs that are widely attributed to Celtic cultures, especially Ireland, yet can be traced to English fairy belief, American fairy belief, or modern popculture. I am choosing in this work to respect the way that people self-identify a belief rather than dissect its actual ultimate source.

3. For example, the term 'spirits' is too vague and would include a range of things like ghosts that are not intended to be included here, while the currently popular term 'fae' is often (erroneously) viewed as a new term and not taken seriously by some groups. Ultimately there is no perfect term free of controversy at the moment so I am making a choice to use fairy, while being fully aware of the difficulty with the word.

4. If the subject of the world of Fairy interests you, as its too big a topic to get into fully here, I do have a book just on that subject *Fairy: The Otherworld by Many Names*

5. *Aos Sidhe* is a notable exception, as that was written to look specifically at Irish beliefs around the Good Folk.

6. Note that current theories suggest this expansion was cultural not migratory.

7. An indigenous American example of this would be the way that the Cherokee brought their beliefs in the Yundwi Tsunsdi and Nunnihe with them when they were forced to go to Oklahoma.

8. In most stories the luxury is replaced with eth exact opposite, and the midwife finds herself in a dim and musty cave rather than a well-appointed mansion.

9. See page 69 of Woodyard & Young's Three *Notes and a Handlist of North American Fairies* for detailed accounts.

10. I encourage people to read Rieti's book as it explores a topic that is currently very popular, the overlap between fairies and UFO phenomena, through the lens of fairy folklore.

11. Alternately in one account the person being interviewed said the bread was to feed the fairies, presumably to gain their favour so they wouldn't harm you.

12. In Inverness, Nova Scotia.

13. It also appears as Hobmen and Hobthrust.

14. Hole in this instance indicating a habitation.

15. The census records 212 entries for the US; I am choosing to exclude two of those as they are third person accounts and incorporate some potential anachronisms. These two date from the 1930s and 1950s respectively and are stories passed down in families.

16. Including Alaska and Hawaii.

17. * The story is included, briefly, in the 1938 book *Connecticut: A Guide to Its Roads, Lore, and People*, page 460.

18. Verdicts in cases of people murdered as changelings varied widely, with the murderer's belief in fairies sometimes taken into account and other times dismissed.

19. Scots-Irish is a term which refers to protestants from the Northern counties of Ireland who immigrated to the US in the 18th and 19th centuries, usually coming from communities which were themselves Scottish transplants to Ireland in the 17th century.

20. I will note here that Brandon Weston makes a point that the word fairy is a newer term in these areas which would not have been used in previous generations, where little people was the common term. The two are now understood as synonymous but were previously distinct.

21. A boggart isn't a Celtic fairy, rather its English, however, I am including it here as a fairy encounter because of its

nebulous nature and as evidence of the range of European influenced beliefs found in the US.

22. It must be noted that newspaper stories of this time period were not necessarily accurate news, and might be fictitious. However, they nonetheless represent strains of wider folk belief which they were usually playing into or mocking and as such are being included here as examples within the body of folklore that existed at the time.

23. I feel obligated to note here that I have had a bean sidhe experience in the US myself as well. This occurred in late 2020, and was a strange shrieking howl which woke both myself and my ex-husband up. I have never heard anything like it before or since. It preceded a very rare local earthquake, which, of course, has no relation to bean sidhe folklore but which I note to give the fullest picture of the experience.

24. They are currently preparing to release a second fairy census, gathered between 2019 and 2023.

25. This is particularly worth noting in relation to the salamander which is envisioned as a kind of fiery amphibian creature but which Paracelsus saw as humanoid.

26. I am expressing no judgment on this belief, before people jump to assume any, simply tracing the available evidence for the source of the belief.

27. This section is an edited and simplified version of a longer essay that appears in my book *A New Dictionary of Fairies*.

28. For example, Isaiah 34:14: "The wild beasts of the desert shall also meet with the wild beasts of the island, and the satyr shall cry to his fellow; the screech owl also shall rest there, and find for herself a place of rest." – KJV Bible.

29. In fairness, he did seem to later pull back from this description and it's an open-ended debate as to whether his ultimate intention was for his elves to have pointed ears or not.

30. The Tuatha Dé Danann are often understood as the old gods of Ireland but also in some belief as the Aos Sidhe or fairy folk.
31. Discussed in Chapter 3.

Bibliography

Alexander, (2023) From Spain to the Americas: tracing the journey of Duendes through cultural traditions. Retrieved from https://gazetteday.com/what-are-duendes/

Atsma, A., (2017) Satyroi http://www.theoi.com/Georgikos/Satyroi.html

Barrett, H., (2019) 'We're Still in Wexford' Says Irish Folklorist Living in Branch. Retrieved from https://www.cbc.ca/news/canada/newfoundland-labrador/we-are-still-in-wexford-irish-folklorist-branch-1.5138239

Blavatsky, H., (1893) Elementals Retrieved from https://www.theosophy.world/resource/elementals-hp-blavatsky

Bovey, A., (2006) Monsters and Grotesques in Medieval Manuscripts

Boyer, D., (2004) Once Upon a Hex

Briggs, K., (1976) A Dictionary of Fairies

Butler, G., (1991) *'The Lutin in French-Newfoundland Culture: Discourse and Belief'*, The Good People: New Fairylore Essays

Castro, R., (2000) Chicano Folklore: a guide to the folktales, traditions, rituals, and religious practices of Mexican-Americans

Cone, S., (1858) The Fairies in America

Cutchin, J., (2015) A Trojan Feast

– – –.(2018) Thieves in the Night

Daimler, M., (2023) *"Irish-American Folk Magic"*, North American Folk Magic

Dunkerson, C., (2017) Do the Elves in Tolkien's Stories Have Pointed Ears? http://tolkien.slimy.com/essays/Ears.html

Evans-Wentz, W., (1911) Fairy Faith in Celtic Countries

Farmer, S., (1894) Folk-Lore of Marblehead, Mass. Retrieved from https://doi.org/10.2307/532844

Federal Writer's Project for the State of Connecticut (1938) Connecticut: A Guide to Its Roads, Lore, and People. Retrieved from https://archive.org/details/connecticut00federich

Fortune, M., (2019) Folklorist Michael Fortune – From Wexford to Newfoundland. Retrieved from https://www.rte.ie/culture/2019/0725/1049421-folklorist-michael-fortune-from-wexford-to-newfoundland/

Fraser, M., (1975) The Folklore of Nova Scotia

Gilly, S., (2019) 'The Fair Folk'; Tales from Appalachia, retrieved from https://mountainlore.net/2019/02/23/the-fair-folk/

Gundarsson, K (2007) Elves, Wights, and Trolls

Hall, A., (2007) Elves in Anglo-Saxon England

Jackson, W., (2017) What Are the Unicorns and Satyrs in the Bible?

Johnson, M., (2014) Seeing Fairies

KJV (2017) Official King James Bible online https://www.kingjamesbibleonline.org/

Lang, A., and Kirk, R., (1893) The Secret Commonwealth of Elves, Fauns, and Fairies

Lavelle, K., (2013) Los Duendes, retrieved from http://folklore.usc.edu/los-duendes/

Leonard, A., (2022) Appalachian Folklore part 2: Sprites and Spirits. Retrieved from https://thekayseean.com/life-and-culture/appalachian-folklore-part-2-sprites-and-spirits/

Lopez, C., (2022) Haunting Story – The Duende (Elves) In Mexico. Retrieved from https://medium.com/@cheniliz.lopez/haunting-story-the-duendes-elves-in-mexico-783420b64dd3

Martineau, J., ed (1998) Victorian Fairy Paintings

McLarty, M., (2022) Behind the Fairy Door: A Look at Fairy Lore in Nova Scotia. Retrieved from www.cbc.ca/news/canada/nova-scotia/behind-the-fairy-door-documentary-1.6574769

México Desconocido (2023) Chaneques, the mischievous Mexican elves. Retrieved from https://www.mexicodesconocido.com.mx/chaneques-duendes-mexicanos.html

Mikl, A., (2004) Fairy Paintings in 19th Century Art and Late 20th Century Art: A Comparative Study http://www2.uwstout.edu/content/lib/thesis/2004/2004mikla.pdf

Munson, M., (2021) The Fairies in Cape Breton

Narvaez, P., (1991) *'Newfoundland Berry Pickers "In the Fairies"; Maintaining Spatial, Temporal, and Moral Boundaries in Legendry'*; The Good People: New Fairylore Essays

Paracelsus (nd) Tractatus IV Retrieved from https://theomagica.com/blog/paracelsus-wisdom-on-the-ecosystem-of-spirits

Purkiss, D., (2000) At the Bottom of the Garden: A Dark History of Fairies, Hobgoblins, and Other Troublesome Things

Quin, E., (2009) Irish American Folklore in New England

Randolph, V., (1947) Ozark Magic and Folklore

Rehder, J., (1992) *"The Scotch-Irish and English in Appalachia."* To Build in a New Ethnic Landscapes in North America

Rieti, B., (1991) Strange Terrain: The Fairy World in Newfoundland

— (1991) *"The Blast in Newfoundland Fairy Tradition"*; The Good People: New Fairylore Essays

Rodriguez, A., (2017) Old Testament Demonology

Schreiwer, R., (2014) The First Book of Urglaawe Myths: Old Deitsch Tales for the Current Era

Silver, C., (1999) Strange & Secret Peoples: Fairies and the Victorian Consciousness

Talirach-Veilmas, L., (2014) Fairy Tales, Natural History and Victorian Culture

Theosophy World (2023) Fairies Retrieved from https://www.theosophy.world/encyclopedia/fairies

Vallee, J., (1969) Passport to Magonia

Weston, B., (2021) Fairy Faith in the Ozarks. Retrieved from www.llewellyn.com/journal/article/2871

White, E., (2014) An Interview with Dr Jenny Butler. Retrieved from https://ethandoylewhite.blogspot.com/2014/01/an-interview-with-dr-jenny-butler.html

Willard, T., (2020) The Monsters of Paracelsus Retrieved from https://www.academia.edu/83978616/The_Monsters_of_Paracelsus

Wimberly, L., (1965) Folklore in the English & Scottish Ballads

Wood, C., (2000) Fairies in Victorian Art

Woodyard, C., (2023) Haunted Ohio Blog, Retrieved from http://hauntedohiobooks.com/category/news/fortean-mysteries/fairies-and-elemental-spirits/

Woodyard, C., and Young, S., (2019) *Three Notes and a Handlist of North American Fairies*, Supernatural Studies, number 6 issue 1

Wright, A., (2009) Puck Through the Ages https://www.boldoutlaw.com/puckrobin/puckages.html

Yeats, W., (1902) Celtic Twilight

Young, S., (2018) Fairy Census. Retrieved from http://www.fairyist.com/wp-content/uploads/2014/10/The-Fairy-Census-2014-2017-1.pdf

About the Author

Morgan Daimler is a blogger, poet, teacher of esoteric subjects, witch, and priestess of the Daoine Maithe. Morgan is a prolific pagan writer, having published more than a dozen books under Moon Books alone, and she is one of the world's foremost experts on all things Fairy. She lives in Connecticut, USA.

SELECTED TITLES

Norse Mythology
Odin
Thor
Freya
Pantheon – The Norse

Fairy Lore
Fairies
Fairycraft
Aos Sidhe
Fairy Witchcraft
21st Century Fairy
A New Dictionary of Fairies
Fairy – The Otherworld by Many Names

Irish Mythology
Lugh
The Dagda
The Morrigan
Irish Paganism
Raven Goddess
Manannán mac Lir
Gods and Goddesses of Ireland

You may also like

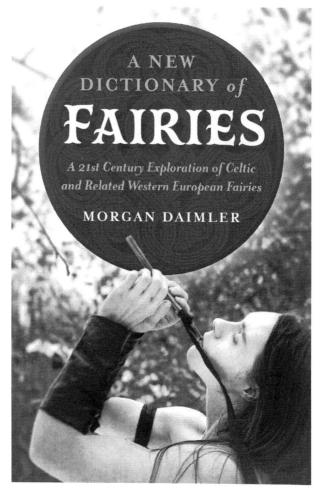

978-1-78904-036-4 (Paperback)
978-1-78904-037-1 (e-book)

MOON BOOKS
PAGANISM & SHAMANISM

What is Paganism? A religion, a spirituality, an alternative belief system, nature worship? You can find support for all these definitions (and many more) in dictionaries, encyclopaedias, and text books of religion, but subscribe to any one and the truth will evade you. Above all Paganism is a creative pursuit, an encounter with reality, an exploration of meaning and an expression of the soul. Druids, Heathens, Wiccans and others, all contribute their insights and literary riches to the Pagan tradition. Moon Books invites you to begin or to deepen your own encounter, right here, right now.

If you have enjoyed this book, why not tell other readers by posting a review on your preferred book site.

Readers of ebooks can buy or view any of these bestsellers by clicking on the live link in the title. Most titles are published in paperback and as an ebook. Paperbacks are available in traditional bookshops. Both print and ebook formats are available online.

Find more titles and sign up to our readers' newsletter
www.collectiveinkbooks.com/paganism

For video content, author interviews and more, please subscribe to our YouTube channel.

MoonBooksPublishing

Follow us on social media for book news, promotions and more:

Facebook: Moon Books

Instagram: @MoonBooksCI

X: @MoonBooksCI

TikTok: @MoonBooksCI